Sexual Offences Against Children in India

Sexual Offences Against Children in India examines the evolution of the law pertaining to sexual violence against children, the judicial decisions since the inception of the POCSO Act till date with respect to aspects of the POCSO Act and the best practices from other developed jurisdictions for handling cases and victims of child abuse.

Despite being prevalent, violence against children is often hidden or under-reported, though its impact is widely acknowledged. In a country like India the vocabulary to communicate around sexuality and sexual abuse is almost non-existent. India has seen its journey from having no law on sexual abuse of children to having a "special" law in the form of the Protection of Children against Sexual Offences Act 2012 (POCSO Act). This book demystifies the problem of sexual violence against children in India pre- and post-POCSO Act. There is also a novel attempt to examine the implementation of the POCSO Act in the eastern Indian states of Odisha, Jharkhand and West Bengal, and if its objectives were being attained – in content, in implementation, and in impact.

This book will be useful for police, judiciary and government officials, scholars, and researchers studying comparative aspects of dealing with sexual offence cases against children.

Sonali Swetapadma is working as an Assistant Professor in the School of Law, KIIT-DU. She has completed her graduation in B.Com (Management) from Ravenshaw University. Thereafter she completed her LLB (Hons) from Madhusudan Law College and her Masters in Law with specialization in Criminal and Security Law from School of Law, KIIT-DU. Currently, she is also pursuing her Ph.D. on the topic "A critical analysis of the Protection of Children against Sexual Offences Act 2012 (with special reference to Odisha)" in KIIT-DU. She has the experience of working as Field Investigator for Odisha in an ICSSR-sponsored Research Programme "Response to the Offence of Rape by the Criminal Justice System – An Empirical Study in the States of Odisha, Jharkhand and West Bengal."

Paromita Chattoraj is a Professor of Law at the National Law University Odisha (NLUO). She graduated with LLB (Hons) from the Department of

Law, University of Calcutta, and completed her LLM, with having specialization in Criminal Law, with a Gold Medal in 2004. She completed her PhD on the subject of Rape Laws in 2013. She worked at the School of Law, KIIT-DU, before joining NLUO. She was a criminal lawyer practising at Calcutta High Court before coming to academics. She had been the recipient of the ICSSR grant in 2013–14 for data Collection in California, USA, for comparative research on Rape Investigation and Prosecution in India and USA. She has been involved with research projects, viz., International Self-Reported Delinquency Project (ISRD-3) from 2012 to 2015 and Major Research Program 2018–20 on Investigation and Trial of Rape cases in the States of Odisha, Jharkhand and West Bengal funded by the ICSSR.

Routledge Frontiers of Criminal Justice

Impending Challenges to Penal Moderation in France and Germany
A Strained Restraint
Edited by Kirstin Drenkhahn, Fabien Jobard and Tobias Singelnstein

Narratives on Prison Governmentality
No Longer the Prison of the Past
Marco Nocente

Preventing Prison Violence
An Ecological Perspective
Armon J. Tamatea, Andrew J. Day and & David J. Cooke

European Perspectives on Pre-Trial Detention
A Means of Last Resort
Christine Morgenstern, Walter Hammerschick and Mary Rogan

War as Protection and Punishment
Armed Military Interventions at the "End of History"
Teresa Degenhardt

Criminalising Coercive Control
Challenges for the Implementation of Northern Ireland's Domestic Abuse Offence
Edited by Vanessa Bettinson and Ronagh McQuigg

Restorative Justice at a Crossroads
Dilemmas of Institutionalisation
Edited by Giuseppe Maglione, Ian D. Marder and Brunhilda Pali

The Lived Experiences of Claiming Wrongful Conviction in Prison
Maintaining Innocence
Emma Burtt

Sexual Offences Against Children in India
Understanding the Criminal Justice Responses
Sonali Swetapadma and Paromita Chattoraj

For more information about this series, please visit: www.routledge.com/Routledge-Frontiers-of-Criminal-Justice/book-series/RFCJ

Sexual Offences Against Children in India

Understanding the Criminal Justice Responses

**Sonali Swetapadma
and Paromita Chattoraj**

Routledge
Taylor & Francis Group

LONDON AND NEW YORK

First published 2024
by Routledge
4 Park Square, Milton Park, Abingdon, Oxon OX14 4RN

and by Routledge
605 Third Avenue, New York, NY 10158

Routledge is an imprint of the Taylor & Francis Group, an informa business

© 2024 Sonali Swetapadma and Paromita Chattoraj

The right of Sonali Swetapadma and Paromita Chattoraj to be identified as authors of this work has been asserted in accordance with sections 77 and 78 of the Copyright, Designs and Patents Act 1988.

British Library Cataloguing-in-Publication Data
A catalogue record for this book is available from the British Library

Library of Congress Cataloging-in-Publication Data
Names: Swetapadma, Sonali, author. | Chattoraj, Paromita, author.
Title: Sexual offences against children in India: understanding the criminal justice responses / Sonali Swetapadma and Paromita Chattoraj.
Description: Abingdon, Oxon; New York, NY: Routledge, 2024. |
Series: Routledge frontiers of criminal justice | Includes bibliographical references and index.
Identifiers: LCCN 2023047856 (print) | LCCN 2023047857 (ebook) |
ISBN 9781032384733 (hardback) | ISBN 9781032384740 (paperback) |
ISBN 9781003345244 (ebook)
Subjects: LCSH: Child sexual abuse–India. | India. Protection of Children from Sexual Offences Act, 2012 | Children–Legal status, laws, etc.–India.
Classification: LCC HV6570.4.I43 S94 2021 (print) | LCC HV6570.4.I43 (ebook) | DDC 362.760954–dc23/eng/20231012
LC record available at https://lccn.loc.gov/2023047856
LC ebook record available at https://lccn.loc.gov/2023047857

ISBN: 978-1-032-38473-3 (hbk)
ISBN: 978-1-032-38474-0 (pbk)
ISBN: 978-1-003-34524-4 (ebk)

DOI: 10.4324/9781003345244

Typeset in Times New Roman
by Deanta Global Publishing Services, Chennai, India

For my father Late Shri Dilip Kumar Chattaraj

Contents

Figures

Tables

List of Cases

	Name of the case	Citation
1.	*Ali Imam vs. The State of West Bengal & Anr.*	*Ali Imam vs. The State of West Bengal & Anr*, decided on August 1, 2022 (High Court of West Bengal)
2.	*Anokhilal vs. State of Madhya Pradesh*	*(2019)20 Supreme Court Cases 196*
3.	*Ashik Ramjan Ansari vs. State of Maharashtra*	*Ashik Ramjan Ansari vs. The State of Maharashtra (CRIMINAL APPEAL NO.1184 OF 2019, High Court of Maharashtra at Bombay*
4.	*Attorney General for India versus Satish and another*	*Attorney General for India versus Satish and another, LL 2021 SC 656)*
5.	*Atul Gorakhnath Ambale vs. The State of Maharashtra*	Criminal Bail Application No. 3242 Of 2019
6.	*Baneshwar Marandi @ Boneshwar vs. The State of Jharkhand*	*Baneshwar Marandi @ Boneshwar vs. The State of Jharkhand* on December 4, 2018 (High Court of Jharkhand)
7.	*Murmu @ Galu vs. State of Odisha*	Bhalu Murmu @ Galu vs. State of Odisha, decided on August 5, 2021 (High Court of Odisha)
8.	*Bhupinder Sharma vs. State of Himachal Pradesh*	(2003) 8 SCC 551
9.	*Bipin Bhoi vs. State of Odisha*	*Bipin Bhoi vs. State of Odisha*, decided on July 22, 2021 (High Court of Odisha)
10.	*Commissioner, Trade Tax, Uttar Pradesh vs. M/S Malkhan S. Subhash Chandra*	Criminal Appeal No. 1581 of 2009
11.	*Gulu Santra @ Ghunu Santra vs. The State of West Bengal*	*Gulu Santra @ Ghunu Santra vs. The State of West Bengal*, decided on June 12, 2020 (High Court of West Bengal)
12.	*Harsh Vibhore Singhal vs. Union of India & Ors*	WRIT PETITION (CIVIL) NO. 000700 OF 2023, Supreme Court of India
13.	*Independent Thought vs. Union of India*	[2017] 10 SCC 800, AIR 2017 SC 4904
14.	*Jagjeet Singh and Ors. vs. Ashish Mishra @ Monu and anr*	Criminal Appeal No. 632 of 2022
15.	*Justin vs. Union of India*	WP (C) No. 15564 of 2017 (U)

Acknowledgements

This book is a culmination of years of thinking about issues surrounding children and being intellectually influenced by the teachings and stimulating discussions with my PhD Supervisors and teachers Prof. V.D. Sebastian and Prof. Bhavani Prasad Panda.

Furthermore, this book is a part of the doctoral research of my co-author Ms Sonali Swetapadma who has worked tirelessly in writing each of the chapters with me and working and re-working until they were able to convey the intended message as I had conceived.

I would also like to thank my LLM student Ms. Pragnyasa Swain, who sincerely helped in collecting the judicial cases under the POCSO Act.

The case studies presented in the book are from the results of the data collection in the Major Research Program entitled "*Response to the Offence of Rape by the Criminal Justice System – An Empirical Study in the States of Odisha, Jharkhand and West Bengal*" granted by the Indian Council for Social Sciences Research (ICSSR) for 2018-2020, Grant no. Gen-35/2017-18/ICSSR/RP. I would also express my gratitude to Prof. Rabi Narayan Subudhi, who was the co-project Director in the above project for supporting with the data analysis of the field data.

I wish to thank my collaborators and good friends from USA, Judge Rupa Goswami and Prof. Paula Mitchell, who exposed me to the California Criminal Justice System giving me invaluable insights of how the offence of rape and CSA is responded by the US system.

On the personal front I would like to thank my father who always taught me to stand by the weak and the marginalized and stand against injustice. I want to thank my mother who is strength personified and who taught me to never give up on my dreams. I am thankful to my two talented teenage daughters who always help me to capture the perspective of today's generation. I am mostly inspired by my husband to always set a higher benchmark for myself and for making me believe that human potential is indeed infinite. My pranam to Ma Sharada for giving me patience and Swami Vivekananda for giving me courage for every endeavour in my life. Finally, I surrender to my ishta devata (Thakur Ramakrishna Paramahansa) as it is he who is doing everything, I am just his instrument.

Prof. Paromita Chattoraj

List of abbreviations

AIR	All India Report
anr.	another
BLJ	Bihar Law Journal
BNS	Bharatiya Nyaya Sanhita
BNSS	Bharatiya Nagarik Suraksha Sanhita
BRIS	Child Rights in Society
BSB	Bharatiya Sakhshya Bill
CANRA	Child Abuse and Neglect Reporting Act
CAPTA	Child Abuse Prevention and Treatment Act
CAST	Child Abuse Services Team
CCL	Centre for Child and Law
CEOP	Child Exploitation and Online Protection
CODIS	Combined DNA Indexing System
CPCR	Commissions for Protection of Child Rights
CRC	Convention on the Rights of the Child
CRCVC	Canadian Resource Centre for Victims of Crime
CrPC	Criminal Procedure Code
CSA	Child Sexual Abuse
CWC	Child Welfare Committees
DLSA	District Legal Services Authority
DVCS	District Victim Compensation Scheme
FIR	First Information Report
FSL	Forensic Science Laboratory
IEA	Indian Evidence Act
IGMSY	Indira Gandhi Matritva Sahyog Yojna
IO	Investigating Officer
IPC	Indian Penal Code
IT Act	Information Technology Act
JH	Jharkhand
MUFSC	Marshall University Forensic Science Centre
MWCD	Ministry of Women and Child Development
NCA	National Crime Agency

NCPCR	National Commission for the Protection of Child Rights
NCRB	National Crime Records Bureau
NCT	National Capital Territory
NGO	Non-Governmental Organisation
NHM	National Health Mission
NLSIU	National Law School of India University
No.	number
NSPCC	National Society for the Prevention of Cruelty to Children
OD	Odisha
OSC	One Stop Centres
POCSO Act	Protection of Children against Sexual Offences Act
PTSD	Post-Traumatic Stress Disorder
RMP	Registered Medical Practitioner
s.	section
SAFE	Sexual Assault Forensic Examination
SANE	Sexual Assault Nurse Examiner
SART	Sexual Assault Response Team
SC	Supreme Court
SCC	Supreme Court Cases
SCPCR	State Commission for the Protection of Child Rights
SJPU	Special Juvenile Police Units
SLSA	State Legal Services Authority
SPP	Special Public Prosecutors
UKHL	United Kingdom House of Lords
UN	United Nation
UNCRC	United Nation Convention on the Rights of the Child
US	United States
USA	United States of America
UT	Union Territory
VCS	Victim Compensation Scheme
vs.	versus
WB	West Bengal
WP (Crl.)	Writ Petition (Criminal)
WP(C)	Writ Petition (Civil)

1 Sexual offences against children and the POCSO Act 2012

Introduction

Violence against children is a global phenomenon affecting all nations. Statistics reveals that at least three out of four children amounting to about 1.7 billion children have experienced cruelty or abuse or some form of violence and exploitation, in their daily lives in a previous year. This impact on children is irrespective of whether they are located in rich or poor countries.[1] Based on the Crime in India Statistics of 2021 published by the National Crime Records Bureau (NCRB), 99.05% of the child victims under the Protection of Children against Sexual Offences Act (POCSO) 2012 are girls.[2] Perpetration of any form of violence is an attack on the dignity and rights of children and eliminates them to experience a normal childhood. Such violence on children affects learning capacities, which in turn puts financial and human costs on individuals as well as societies.[3] The issue of sexual abuse of children is prevalent in every pocket of India, in every age group of children belonging to all socio-economic classes and of both the genders. In India, 21% of the children have faced severe sexual abuse and at least half of them have faced some form of sexual abuse, in their lives.[4]

Violence against children is kept under wraps, invisible or definitely under-reported, despite its high prevalence. In a country where vocabulary surrounding sex and sexuality is taboo, the narratives around sexuality and sexual abuse are almost non-existent. The definition of Child Sexual Abuse (CSA) was formulated by the 1999 World Health Organisation Consultation on Child Abuse Prevention, which stated,

> Child Sexual Abuse is the involvement of a child in sexual activity that he or she does not fully comprehend, is unable to give informed consent to, or for which the child is not developmentally prepared and cannot give consent, or that violates the laws or social taboos of society.[5]

Child sexual abuse is said to occur when the activity between a child and an adult or another child who by age or development is more mature or in a

DOI: 10.4324/9781003345244-1

position of trust or power, where the activity is intended to gratify or satisfy the needs of the adult or the other person. This may include but is not limited to

- the inducement or coercion of a child to engage in any unlawful sexual activity;
- the exploitative use of a child in prostitution or other unlawful sexual practices; and
- the exploitative use of children in pornographic performance and materials.[6]

Of note, these definitions include acts that both do and do not involve physical touching or physical force, including completed sexual acts, attempted sexual acts, abusive sexual touching, and non-contact assaults such as harassment, threats, forced exposure to pornography, and taking unwanted sexual images, such as filming or photography. In some instances, the recipient may not be aware of their own victimization or that violence has been perpetrated against them. This breadth of scope reflects the recognition that imposing sexual intent of any sort on someone against his or her will on a child is an inherently violent act, regardless of the use of physical force or resulting contact or injury.

Sexual abuse of children is a serious problem of considerable magnitude throughout the world. Children, under the age of 18, contribute to 37% of India's population.[7] Until recently, it was not statutorily acknowledged as a criminal offence in India. Rape, which is a gendered offence and recognized only against females, was the main, if not the only, specific sexual offence against the girl child. In the absence of specific legislation, a range of offensive behaviours such as child sexual assault (not amounting to rape), harassment, and exploitation for pornography were never criminalized. Non-Governmental Organizations (NGOs) and the Central Government's Ministry of Women and Child Development were actively engaged for breaking "the conspiracy of silence" and have generated substantial political and popular momentum to address the issue.[8] This led to an increased activism around child protection in the media and public discourse. This movement spearheaded by the Ministry of Women and Child Development led to the enactment of new legislation called the Protection of Children against Sexual Offences Act 2012 (hereinafter, the POCSO Act)".

Table 1.1 explains the gravity of the problem of child sexual abuse in India, where the highest number of cases involved girl victims from 16 to 18 years, the figures for victims less than 6 years is also distressing. Although the ratio of boy child victims to girl child victims is minimal, the figures are alarming.

Prior to the enactment of the POCSO Act 2012, the cases of sexual abuse of children were dealt under the Indian Penal Code (IPC) and some sections of the Information Technology Act, 2000 under the following heads:

Table 1.1 Age profile of victims of POCSO in India[9]

Year	Less than 6 years		6–12 years		12–16 years		16–18 years	
	Boy	**Girl**	**Boy**	**Girl**	**Boy**	**Girl**	**Boy**	**Girl**
2021	25	650	140	3157	83	13173	69	16206
2020	18	622	145	2395	80	10949	26	14092
2019	23	686	113	2514	97	9318	35	13711
2018	18	675	94	2211	100	8569	17	10393
2017	17	639	75	2089	71	6603	20	8266

Note: This table has been compiled by the author.

- Sections 292[10] and 293[11] of IPC deal with obscenity generally but not with "Online Obscenity." In *Ranjit D. Udeshi vs. State of Maharashtra,*[12] the Supreme Court held that pornography is obscenity in a more aggravated form.
- Section 372 IPC[13]: Selling of minor children for purpose of prostitution.
- Section 375[14] and 376 IPC[15]: Rape (including girl child) and punishment of rape.
- Section 377 IPC[16]: Unnatural Offence: This provision being gender neutral used to be invoked in any case of child sexual abuse involving a boy.
- Section 67B of Information Technology (IT) Act, 2000[17] took care of online abuse of a child and even transmitting or publishing any sexually exploitative content of the child was punishable under this section.

There were no specific laws in India to address sexual offences against children effectively. Therefore, the major shortcomings that prompted the need for a special legislation to deal with cases of sexual offences against children may be summarized as follows:

1. Provisions of the Indian Penal Code, 1860 were not gender neutral, for example: Sections 375 and 376 were only concerned with the female child, and the male child was left out.
2. The different degrees of sexual assault on children were not captured by the existing laws.
3. Different surveys conducted by the Government of India showed the need for a specific law to deal with sexual offences against children.[18]
4. In case of abuse by a family member, such questions remained unanswered.
5. Despite provisions in the Information and Technology Act, 2000 that dealt with child pornography, they were not effective enough to stop online child abuse.

The only exception was the state of Goa, where child abuse charges were solely prosecuted under the Goa Children's Act 2003 until the POSCO Act 2012 was introduced,[19] which had provided for specific protection of children. The Goa Act had been one of the only Indian statutes, which provided the legal definition of trafficking too, with regard to child-specific calls.

Hence, in this light the need for POCSO Act was felt and the same came into force.

International conventions on child sexual abuse and protection of the rights of the child

United Nations Convention on the Rights of the Child

Since its adoption by the United Nations General Assembly in 1989, the Convention on the Rights of the Child (CRC) has become the first binding instrument in international law concerning the rights of children, and the most universally ratified human rights treaty in history[20]. One of the most important international agreements is the UNCRC (UN Convention on the Rights of the Child, adopted in 1989). The Convention on the Rights of the Child recognises children and adolescents as legal subjects in their own right. Children's rights are grouped into participation, promotion and protection rights.

Articles 19 and 34 are especially important for protecting children and adolescents from sexual violence. Article 19 governs the obligation of countries to protect children from all forms of violence, which includes sexual violence. Under Article 34 of the UNCRC, countries must explicitly commit to protecting children from all forms of sexual exploitation and sexual abuse. The UNCRC has been broadened by the addition of three more protocols in the meantime. The second of these protocols governs other rights of children, which concern the selling of children, child prostitution and depictions of abuse, i.e. so-called child pornography. The signatory countries must report back to the UN Committee on the Rights of the Child once every five years about how they have implemented the UNCRC in their own country.

Lanzarote Convention

The Council of Europe Convention for the protection of children against sexual exploitation and sexual abuse was adopted and opened for signature on 25 October 2007 in Lanzarote, Spain. For this reason, it is otherwise known as the Lanzarote Convention. The Lanzarote Convention entered into force on 1 July 2010.[21] Till date, it has been ratified by all forty-six Council of Europe member states and two non-member states, namely the Russian Federation and Tunisia. Any non-member State of the Council of Europe may request accession to the Lanzarote Convention. Tunisia was the first non-member State to accede to the Lanzarote Convention. The Committee of Ministers of the Council of Europe also agreed to accept such a request by the Kingdom of Morocco, which has not yet deposited its instrument of accession.[22]

The Council of Europe Convention on Protection of Children against Sexual Exploitation and Sexual Abuse, requires criminalisation of all kinds of sexual offences against children. It sets out that states in Europe and beyond shall adopt specific legislation and take measures to prevent sexual violence, to protect child victims and to prosecute perpetrators.

The Lanzarote Convention is the most ambitious and comprehensive international (potentially universal) legal instrument on the protection of children against sexual exploitation and sexual abuse. Its drafters took as a starting point the relevant United Nations and Council of Europe standards, extending them to cover all possible kinds of sexual offences against children (including sexual abuse of a child, exploitation of children through prostitution, and grooming and corruption of children through exposure to sexual content and activities and offences related to child abuse material).[23] The Convention covers sexual abuse within the *circle of trust*, namely in the child's family or by other people with whom children have a relationship of trust, as well as acts carried out for commercial or profit-making purposes. It sets forth that the states in Europe and beyond shall establish specific legislation to criminalize such behaviour and take measures with an emphasis on keeping the best interest of children at the forefront, not only to prevent sexual violence but also to protect child victims and prosecute perpetrators. It also promotes international cooperation to achieve the such objectives.

Some of the countries have enacted victim-specific legislations that enlarged the scope of participation by the victims and also expanded the ambit of victims' rights. Victims Crime Act, 1984, Victims' Rights and Restitution Act, 1990 were enacted by the United States of America to grant legal assistance to the crime-victims. With similar purposes, Australia enacted South Australian Victims of Crime Act, 2001 and Canada enacted the Canadian Victims Bill of Rights.

Background on the evolution of the POCSO Act

Time and again various recommendations have been made to strengthen the laws relating to trial and investigation of rape cases and also the position of the victims in the criminal justice system. Such recommendations can be broadly classified under the heads of victim's participation, assistance, and restoration. A report of some of the key Law Commissions and other committees specifically addressed the issues on sexual offences and victims' position and recommended changes in the legal framework. The 154th Law Commission Report was titled 'Amendment to the Indian Evidence Act, 1872 – Victims of Sexual Offences and Rape Trials.' The report made several recommendations on victim rights that were later passed into law as part of the Criminal Law (Amendment) Act, 2013. The Malimath Committee was appointed by the Government of India in the year 2000 to review the criminal justice system and make recommendations for its reform. The committee submitted its report in 2003, which contained several recommendations on victim rights.

In its 172nd Law Commission Report on Review of Rape Laws, the Commission recommended for widening the definition of rape in Section 375 of IPC and also making it gender neutral to prevent the crime of sexual abuse against youngsters. The Commission has also recommended the insertion of a new Section 376E dealing with unlawful sexual contact, the deletion of Section 377 of the Indian Penal Code, and the enhancement of punishment in Section 509[24] of the Indian Penal Code. The Commission proposed for substituting the word rape by *sexual assault* in accordance with the suggestions of the National Commission for Women. The Report came out of a petition made by *Sakshi Vs. Union of India*[25] drawing the attention of the Supreme Court to the inability of the present laws relating to rape to cover various sexual violations against women or children.

As an aftermath of a gruesome gangrape that occurred in the capital city of Delhi in December 2012, a three-member committee was constituted, headed by Justice J.S. Verma, former Chief Justice of the Supreme Court, for recommending changes in the Criminal Law for providing effective investigation, swifter trial, more stringent punishment for perpetrators accused of committing sexual offences against women and children, and a more victim-friendly approach as a whole. The Committee made far-reaching recommendations to amend laws related to rape, trafficking, and child sexual abuse, bringing in offences of sexual harassment, procedural safeguards for the victim during reporting, investigation especially medical examination, and police accountability, among other reforms.

Pro-victim recommendations

Some of the key recommendations on victim participation, assistance, and restoration that may be applicable to victims of sexual abuse are discussed below.

Victim participation

1. *Right to be heard*: The 154th Law Commission and the Malimath Committee recommended that victims of sexual offences should have the right to be heard at all stages of the investigation and trial. Also, the victim should be heard during bail proceedings. The Malimath Committee also recommended that victims should be allowed to participate in the trial and cross-examine witnesses, subject to certain conditions. The Verma Committee recommended that victims of sexual offences should have the right to be heard at all stages of the investigation and trial.

The above recommendations were included firstly, as a proviso to Section 24(8) of the CrPC,[26] which enables the victim to have a separate lawyer during trial. However, such a lawyer only plays second fiddle to the prosecutor (representing the state in a criminal trial). Secondly, the victim's counsel has the right to present their questions and arguments through the court under Section 311 CrPC[27] and Section 165[28] of Indian Evidence Act. *Thirdly,* it was included by the 2018 Criminal Law Amendment under s.439(1A) CrPC[29] that provides for the presence of the informant or any person authorised by him/her shall be obligatory at the time of hearing of the application for bail to the person under sub-section (3) of section 376 or section 376AB or section 376DA or section 376DB of the IPC. In this connection the Supreme Court in the case *of Jagjeet Singh and Ors. v. Ashish Mishra @ Monu and anr*[30] clarified that a *"victim and complainant/informant are two distinct connotations in criminal jurisprudence. It is not always necessary that the complainant/ informant is also a 'victim,' for even a stranger to the act of crime can be an 'informant,' and similarly, a 'victim' need not be the complainant or informant of a felony."*

In *Mallikarjun Kodagali (Dead) v. State of Karnataka and ors,*[31] the Supreme Court observed:

> *"The rights of victims, and indeed victimology, is an evolving jurisprudence and it is more than appropriate to move forward in a positive direction, rather than stand still or worse, take a step backward. A voice has been given to victims of crime by Parliament and the judiciary and that voice needs to be heard, and if not already heard, it needs to be raised to a higher decibel so that it is clearly heard."*

In the case of *Jagjeet Singh and ors. v. Ashish Mishra @ Monu and anr,*[32] a three-judge bench held that *"the victims have right to be heard, especially in cases involving heinous crimes; and when the victims themselves come forward to participate in a criminal proceeding."* The court also observed in this case that,

> *"If the right to file an appeal against acquittal, is not accompanied with the right to be heard at the time of deciding a bail application, the same may result in grave miscarriage of justice. Victims certainly cannot be expected to be sitting on the fence and watching the proceedings from afar, especially when they may have legitimate grievances. It is the solemn duty of a court to deliver justice before the memory of an injustice eclipses".*

2. *Right to legal aid*: The 154th Law Commission, the Malimath Committee and The Verma Committee recommended that victims of sexual offences should have access to free legal aid, particularly in cases where the

accused is represented by a lawyer. However, this right is not provided under the CrPC in section 304,[33] which specifically provides for legal aid to the accused but not to the victim. So far, the right to legal aid for victims can only be found under s.12 of the Legal Services Authorities Act 1987.[34]

Victim assistance

1. *Right to speedy trial*: The 154th Law Commission recommended that the investigation and trial of sexual offences should be completed within a specified timeframe. The Malimath Committee recommended that the trial of a case should be completed within a reasonable time, to avoid prolonged suffering of the victim. The Verma Committee also recommended that the investigation and trial of sexual offences should be completed within a specified timeframe. This was included by the Criminal Law Amendment Act of 2018 in Section 309 of the CrPC,[35] which provides for the trial of sexual offences to be completed within two months.

2. *Right to privacy*: The 154th Law Commission recommended that the identity of the victim of a sexual offence should not be disclosed in any manner, including in the media. The Verma Committee also recommended that the identity of the victim should be kept confidential in all cases involving sexual offences. This was given effect by the 1983 amendment under section 228-A IPC,[36] which made it a punishable offence to divulge the identity or print or publish the identity of a victim of sexual offence, and the 2013 Criminal Law Amendment included the new sexual offences against women that are mentioned under section 376-A,[37] 376-AB,[38] 376-B,[39] 376-C,[40] 376-D,[41] 376-DA,[42] 376-DB,[43] and R 376-E.[44] The corresponding provision in the CrPC is s.327(3)[45] CrPC, which bans printing or publication of the identity of the victims of rape and other sexual offences while publishing the trial proceedings.

3. *Right to information*: The Malimath Committee recommended that victims should be informed about the progress of the investigation and the trial and should be provided with copies of relevant documents. However, this has not translated into any legal provision whereby a victim shall be notified about the investigation or trial.

Victim restoration

1. *Right to dignity*: The 154th Law Commission and the Verma Committee recommended that the dignity of the victim should be protected during the investigation and trial of sexual offences. In effect for victims of sexual offences, section 146 in the Indian Evidence Act, 1872,[46] was inserted whereby, in a prosecution for rape and other sexual offences, it shall not be permissible to put questions in the cross-examination of the victim

as to her general immoral character. Furthermore, Clause (4) of Section 155 of the Indian Evidence Act 1872 was repealed, which provided for questioning of the victim's character when a man is prosecuted for rape or an attempt to rape.

2. *Right to rehabilitation*: The 154th Law Commission and the Verma Committee recommended that victims of sexual offences should be provided with medical and psychological care and rehabilitation. The Criminal Law Amendment Act of 2009 inserted s.357C CrPC,[47] which provides that all hospitals, public or private, whether run by the Central Government, the State Government, local bodies or any other person, shall immediately, provide the first-aid or medical treatment, free of cost, to the victims of sexual offences, that may be before filing information with the police.

3. *Right to compensation*: The Malimath Committee recommended that victims should have the right to receive compensation from the state for the harm suffered as a result of the crime. Under section 357(1) and (3) of CrPC[48] victims have a right to get compensation from the accused who caused harm to them. Therefore, section 357A of CrPC[49] was inserted that provides for the establishment of a fund for the rehabilitation of victims of sexual offences by the State.

4. *Medical examination of a rape victim*: The Verma Committee recommended for abolishing the practice of the two-finger test conducted during medical examination to determine the laxity of the vaginal muscles. This has been upheld by the Supreme Court also through various judgements while declaring that the previous sexual experience of the victim should not be a consideration in determining the question of consent or the nature of consent given by the victim. The procedure for conducting the medical examination of a rape victim is provided under section 164A CrPC[50] and s.27 POCSO Act.[51]

These amendments strengthened the rights of victims and made the criminal justice system more responsive to their needs.

The POCSO Act 2012

The POCSO Act, 2012 is a special law that aims at protecting children from all types of sexual offences and at the same time providing special treatment for the child victim by the police as well as the court. Although the Convention on the Rights of the Child was adopted by the United Nations in 1989, the offences against children were not redressed by way of any specific legislation in India till the year 2012. The Act provides for stringent punishments for the offender for the commission of offences against children and at the same time provides for victim-friendly procedures for the child victim of both genders. The POCSO Act, 2012, is divided into 46 sections and it came into force on November 14, 2012.

Salient features of the Act

The salient features of the POCSO Act 2012 are as follows:

- Child according to the Act are those below 18 years and the Act is gender neutral recognizing both young girls and boys as victims.
- The Act provides for mandatory reporting of sexual offences and punishment for failure to report (sections 20 and 21 POCSO Act).
- The Act defines child pornography "as any visual depiction of sexually explicit conduct involving a child, including photographs, video, digital, or computer-generated images indistinguishable from an actual child."
- The Act calls for the establishment of Special Juvenile Police Units (SJPUs) for dealing with cases of sexual abuse of children.
- Presumption of guilt in case of penetrative and non-penetrative sexual assaults under sections 3,5,7, and 9 of the Act.
- Presumption of *culpable state* in all offences under the Act.
- Different forms of sexual abuse have been defined in the Act including but not limited to sexual harassment, pornography, and penetrative and non-penetrative assault.
- The Act recognizes a graver degree of offences in the form of aggravated penetrative or non-penetrative sexual assault. If the child is mentally ill or when the abuse is committed by a person in a position of trusts such as a doctor, teacher, policeman, or family member.
- Child-friendly provisions have been included to deter secondary victimization of the child by institutional stakeholders in the criminal justice system. The policeman has been assigned the role of the child protector during the investigation process.
- The Act provides for the designation of Special Courts for trying sexual offences cases.
- The Act stipulates that the case is disposed of by the court within one year from the date of taking cognizance of the offence.
- To monitor the implementation of the Act, the National Commission for the Protection of Child Rights (NCPCR) and State Commissions for the Protection of Child Rights (SCPCRs) have been designated and also the commissions have the power to make inquiries into child abuse cases under the Act.
- Section 42A provides the overriding effect of the Act in case of inconsistency with provisions of any other law.

- The Act provides for anonymity to the victim against disclosure of his/ her identity under Section 23 of the POCSO Act, unless the Special Court has allowed the disclosure.

Offences defined under the Act

- Penetrative sexual assault: Involving penetration that is peno-vaginal, peno-oral, peno-urethral or peno-anal, fingering or object penetration.
  Punishment: Not less than 10 years; this may extend to life imprisonment, and fine. In case the victim is a child below the age of sixteen, then the imprisonment term shall not be less than twenty years which may extend upto life imprisonment fine or both (Section 4).
- Aggravated penetrative sexual assault: Committed by a person of trust or authority such as a police officer.
  Punishment: Rigorous imprisonment for a term not less than 20 years; which may extend to life imprisonment or death, and a fine (Section 6).
- Sexual assault: Committed by whoever, with a sexual intent, touches the vagina, penis, anus or breast of the child, makes the child touch the vagina, penis, anus or breast of such person or any other person does any other act with sexual intent which involves physical contact without penetration.
  Punishment: Not less than 3 years; this may extend to 5 years, and a fine (Section 8).
- Aggravated non-penetrative sexual assault committed by a person of trust or authority such as a police officer.
  Punishment: Not less than 5 years; this may extend to 7 years, and a fine (Section 10).
- Sexual harassment is defined as unwelcome sexual remarks, emails or telephone calls; taunting, jeering, demands or requests for sexual favours.
  Punishment: imprisonment term up to 3 years and fine (Section 12).
- Use of minor for pornographic purposes involving a child in the preparation, production and/or distribution of pornography via print, electronic, computer or any other technology.
  Punishment: Minimum term of 5 years and fine, and in the event of second conviction, 7 years and a fine (Section 14 (1)).
- Attempt of offence:
  Punishment: Imprisonment for any description provided for the offence, for a term which may extend to one half of the longest term of imprisonment provided for the said offence and with fine or both (Section 18).
- Abetment of offence: Instigating a person to commit an offence; conspiring to commit an offence; intentionally aiding an offence.
  Punishment: Same as that of the offence abetted (Section 17).
- Non-reporting an offence
  Punishment: 6 months and/or a fine (Section 21).

Victim-friendly procedures

The POCSO Act places certain obligations on the stakeholders of the police and court for providing child-friendly procedures for the victim, which are as follows:

- The statement of the child is to be recorded at his/her place of residence and generally by a woman police officer.
- The officer who is to record the statement of the child should not be wearing a uniform.
- The officer should ensure that the child does not come in contact with the accused during the examination.
- A child is not to be detained in the police station at night.
- The officer should ensure that the identity of the child is not revealed.
- The statement of the child is to be recorded in the presence of a person in whom the child has trust, for example, their parents.
- The statement of the child is to be recorded via audio-video electronic means.
- The assistance of the translators or interpreters should be taken wherever necessary.
- Frequent breaks are to be allowed during the trial.
- The special court has to ensure that the child is not called to repeatedly testify in the trial court.
- Aggressive questioning of the child is not permitted during the trial.

Presumption of guilt

The starting premise in criminal jurisprudence is that a person accused of a crime is presumed to be innocent until proven guilty (*Woolmington v. D.P.P)*[52]. The maxim *juris sed non de jure* connotes that facts hold good until contradicted by evidence, which is also known as the general rule of evidence. Since in criminal trial the burden to prove the guilt of the accused is on the prosecution who has levelled the charges, therefore, until the prosecution can successfully prove the guilt, the accused is presumed to be innocent. However, in certain exceptional circumstances the law may presume the guilt of an accused in the larger interests of society and to meet the ends of justice. One such scenario is presented by section 29 of the POCSO Act that enumerates specific offences under the Act, for which the Special Court shall presume that the accused is guilty unless the contrary is proved. This is, therefore, known as the reverse burden in criminal trial.[53]

The presumption of guilt under the POCSO Act was incorporated by the legislature considering the vulnerability of the child victim and other factors such as the inherent grievousness and heinousness of the crime, and unavailability of eyewitness or direct witnesses due to its commission in isolation or behind closed doors in secrecy. The reason for introducing such a provision was due to the child victim's vulnerability and difficulty in collecting evidence that made it necessary to place such an onerous burden on the accused (Parliamentary Standing Committee on Human Resource Development in its 240th Report on the POCSO Bill, 2011).[54]

The provision of reverse burden u/s 29 is effective in cases, firstly, involving those acts of sexual abuse on the child that do not leave any physical marks and in such cases medical examination may not yield any fruitful results. Secondly, cases where the sole but weak testimony of the child on account of immaturity or inexperience or incoherence in the statement of the child witness make the crux of the prosecution's case, and thirdly, in cases where there is a lack of any corroboration through medical reports or by the testimony of any other witnesses.[55]

The Kerala High Court in *Justin v. Union of India*[56] while upholding the constitutionality of reverse burden or onus clause under the POCSO Act stated that

> "*presumption of guilt of an accused commences only once the prosecution has proved "foundational facts" of the case. Foundational facts in a POCSO case include – proof that the victim is a child, that the alleged incident has occurred, and whenever physical injury is caused, supporting it with medical evidence. Thus, only once the court is confident that the alleged act took place does it presume the guilt of the accused and the accused can then rebut this presumption.*"

Role of the National and State Commission for the Protection of Child Rights[57]

The **National Commission for Protection of Child Rights (NCPCR)** is a judicial body founded in 2007 under the Parliament's Commissions for Protection of Child Rights (CPCR) Act, 2005. The POCSO Act makes the NCPCR as the monitoring agency to ensure the proper implementation of the Act and the NCPCR operates under the Ministry of Women & Child Development of the Central Government. The main objective of the NCPCR is to protect, promote, and defend children's rights across the country. Section 17 of the CPCR speaks about the constitution of the State Commission for the Protection of Child Rights. The SCPCRs function on a state-level basis on similar lines to that of the NCPCR. Section 44 of the POCSO Act[58] lays down the responsibility of monitoring the implementation of the Act on the NCPCR or the SCPCR as the case may be. Therefore, the onus lies on the NCPCR/SCPCR to ensure the proper implementation of the POCSO Act at both national and the state level.

Some of the key functions of the National Commission for Protection of Child Rights, as laid out in the Commissions for Protection of Child Rights

(CPCR) Act, 2005 that translate effective functioning of the POCSO Act and better protection of the abused child, are as follows:

1. Inquire into violation of child rights and recommend initiation of proceedings in such cases.
2. Examine all factors that inhibit the enjoyment of rights of children affected by terrorism, communal violence, riots, natural disasters, domestic violence, HIV/AIDS, trafficking, maltreatment, torture and exploitation, pornography, and prostitution and recommend appropriate remedial measures.
3. Look into the matters relating to the children in need of special care and protection including children in distress, marginalized and disadvantaged children, children in conflict with law, juveniles without family, and children of prisoners and recommend appropriate remedial measures.
4. Spread child rights literacy among various sections of society and promote awareness of the safeguards available for the protection of these rights through publications, the media, seminar, and other available means.
5. Inquire into complaints and take *suo motu* notice of the matter relating to
   • Deprivation and violation of child rights.
   • Non-implementation of laws providing for the protection and development of children.
   • Non-compliance of policy decisions, guidelines, or instructions aimed at mitigating hardships to and ensuring the welfare of the children and providing relief to such children.
   • Or take up the issues arising out of such matters with appropriate authorities.
6. Analyse the existing law, policy, and practice to assess compliance with the Convention on the Rights of the Child, undertake inquiries, and produce reports on any aspects of policy or practice affecting children and comment on proposed new legislation related to child rights.
7. Undertake formal investigation where concern has been expressed either by children themselves or by the concerned person on their behalf.
8. Produce and disseminate information about child rights and compile and analyse data on children.
9. Promote the incorporation of child rights into the school curriculum and training of teachers or personnel dealing with children.

Scheme of the chapters

In this book the second chapter is **Criminal justice process from the child victim's lens**, which deals with the impact of sexual offences on victims, including the types of victimization and the phenomenon of victim shaming.

It further discusses the Intersection of the Child Victim of Sexual Offences with the Criminal Justice System and ends with some discussion on the best practices from other countries while handling the victims of sexual abuse in the Criminal Justice System.

The third chapter is **Role of police in investigation of sexual offences against children** and covers the trajectory of the investigation of sexual offence cases generally against children, specifically starting with reporting, recording of statement of the victims, medical examination, and arrest of the accused and concluding with some instances of the best practices of investigation from around the world.

The fourth chapter covers the **Dynamics of trial process in Child Sexual Offence Cases.** In this chapter the authors discuss the role of the Special courts and the judges functioning under the POCSO Act highlighting the victim-friendly obligations on the court mandated by the law, pendency of cases, and compensation and sentencing for sexual offences.

In the second, third, and fourth chapters in addition to the discussion of the laws and best practices, the authors have appropriately included case studies from the results of their empirical research on the investigation and trial of rape and POCSO cases in three states of eastern India, namely, Odisha (OD), West Bengal (WB), and Jharkhand (JH).[59]

The final chapter deals with **Judicial approach in cases under POCSO Act** and covers the judicial cases on different aspects of sexual offence against children viz. reporting of the offence, recording of the statement of the victim, medical examination of the victim, evidentiary value of forensic evidence, victim-friendly proceedings, burden of proof, sentencing, and compensation to the victim.

It is pertinent to mention here that as the authors were finishing this book, the Union home minister introduced three new Bills in the Lok Sabha (the lower house of the Indian Parliament), viz.: the Bharatiya Nyaya Sanhita (BNS) Bill, 2023 to replace the Indian Penal Code, 1860 (IPC); the Bharatiya Nagarik Suraksha Sanhita Bill (BNSS), 2023 to replace the Code of Criminal Procedure, 1898 (CrPC); and the Bharatiya Sakhshya Bill (BSB), 2023 to replace Indian Evidence Act, 1872. The Bills were introduced on the last day of the monsoon session of the parliament, on August 11, 2023, and were subsequently referred to a Select Committee for further deliberation.[60] The laws are yet to be passed and may be further modified from the versions that are present in the Bills. Although the POCSO Act is the special law to deal with cases of child sexual offences, rape of minor girls is also charged under the general substantive law of IPC and provisions of the CrPC and Evidence Act are applied in such cases wherever the special law is silent. Therefore, we have mentioned wherever appropriate any proposed change in these three laws that may have implications on the reporting, investigation, or trial of sexual offences against children.

Notes

1 *CSA in Global Context (Ending Violence in Childhood Global Report 2017)*, ARPAN, January 30, 2020, 12:39. https://www.arpan.org.in/protection-of-children -from-sexual-offences-act-pocso/
2 National Crime Records Bureau, *Age Profile of Child Victims of POCSO Act (State/ UT-wise) – 2021*, 2021. https://ncrb.gov.in/sites/default/files/CII-2021/CII-2021 -Tables.html
3 A. Rawat, "The Juxtaposition of POCSO in Various Countries." *International Journal of Law Management & Humanities*, 4, no. 4 (2021): 2321–2332. https:// doi.org/10.10000/IJLMH.111498
4 Ibid at 1.
5 K. Srivastava, S. Chaudhury, P.S. Bhat and P. Patkar, "Child Sexual Abuse: The Suffering Untold." *Industrial Psychiatry Journal*, 26, no. 1 (2017, January– June): 1–3. https://doi.org/10.4103/ipj.ipj_83_17. PMID: 29456313; PMCID: PMC5810157.
6 R. Seth and R.N. Srivastava, "Child Sexual Abuse: Management and Prevention, and Protection of Children from Sexual Offences (POCSO) Act." *Indian Pediatrics*, 54, no. 11 (2017): 949–953. https://doi.org/10.1007/s13312-017-1189-9
7 Vikas Choudhry et al., "Child Sexual Abuse in India: A Systematic Review." *PLOS ONE*, October 9, 2018, available at https://journals.plos.org/plosone/article/file ?type=printable&id=10.1371/journal.pone.0205086
8 Priya Jagadeesh, "Child Sexual Abuse and the Law in India." *Legalservice India*, January 14, 2020, 11:26. http://www.legalserviceindia.com/legal/article-809-child -sexual-abuse-and-the-law-in-india.html
9 Crime in India Statistics, NCRB.
10 Section 292 IPC: – Sale, etc., of obscene books, etc.
11 Section 293 IPC: – Sale, etc., of obscene objects to young person.
12 Ranjit D. Udeshi vs. State of Maharashtra 1965 AIR 881, 1965 SCR (1) 65.
13 Section 372 IPC: – Selling minor for purposes of prostitution, etc.
14 Section 375 IPC: – Rape.
15 Section 376: – Punishment for rape.
16 Section 377 IPC – Unnatural offences.
17 Section 67B Information Technology Act 2000: Punishment for publishing or trans- mitting of material depicting children in sexually explicit act, etc. in electronic form.
18 Manish Kumawat, "Child Sexual Abuse Laws in India – The POCSO Act." *iPlead- ers*, January 25, 2019, 20:50. https://blog.ipleaders.in/pocso-act/
19 V. Bairwa, "After Effects of Goa's Children Act, 2003." *Jus Corpus Law Journal*. https://cdnbbsr.s3waas.gov.in/s35d6646aad9bcc0be55b2c82f69750387/uploads /2021/10/2021102971.pdf
20 UNICEF, ON THE RIGHTS OF THE CHILD. Available at https://www.unicef. org.uk/what-we-do/un-convention-child-rights/#:~:text=The%20UN%20Conventi on%20on%20the%20Rights%20of%20the%20Child%20(UNCRC,human%20 rights%20treaty%20in%20history (Last visited on 21-12-2023 at 12:08).
21 Lanzarote Convention, available at https://www.coe.int/en/web/children/lanzarote -convention (visited on July 12, 2023).
22 Ibid.
23 T. Kleinsorge, "Legal Protection of Children from Sexual Exploitation: The 'Lanzarote Convention' and the ONE in FIVE Campaign," available at chrome- extension://efaidnbmnnnibpcajpcglclefindmkaj/https://violenceagainstchildren.un .org/sites/violenceagainstchildren.un.org/files/expert_consultations/law_reform/ tanja_klainsorge_legal_protection_of_children_from_sexual_exploitation.pdf.

24 Section 509. IPC-Word, gesture or act intended to insult the modesty of a woman.
25 AIR 2004 SC 3566, 2004 (2) ALD Cri 504.
26 Section 24 Criminal Procedure Code (CrPC) – Public Prosecutors.
27 S. 311 Criminal Procedure Code (CrPC)-
    Power to summon material witness, or examine person present
28 S. 165 Indian Evidence Act 1872- Judge's power to put questions or order production.
29 S. 439 Code of Criminal Procedure (CrPC)- Special powers of High Court or Court of Session regarding bail.
30 Criminal Appeal No. 632 of 2022.
31 (2019) 2 SCC 752
32 Criminal Appeal No. 632 of 2022.
33 S. 304 Code of Criminal Procedure (CrPC).
34 Section 12 Legal Services Authority Act 1987 – Criteria for giving legal services.
35 S. 309 Criminal Procedure Code (CrPC).
36 S. 228A Indian Penal Code (IPC)- Disclosure of identity of the victim of certain offences, etc.
37 S. 376A Indian Penal Code (IPC) – Punishment for causing death or resulting in persistent vegetative state of victim.
38 S. 376 AB Indian Penal Code IPC.
39 S. 376 B Indian Penal Code (IPC) – Sexual intercourse by husband upon his wife during separation.
40 S. 376 C Indian Penal Code (IPC) – Sexual intercourse by person in authority.
41 S. 376 D Indian Penal Code (IPC) – Gang Rape.
42 S. 376 DA Indian Penal Code (IPC) – Punishment for gang rape on woman under sixteen years of age.
43 S. 376 DB Indian Penal Code (IPC) – Punishment for gang rape on woman under 12 years of age.
44 Section 376E Indian Penal Code (IPC): – Punishment for repeat offenders.
45 Section 327 Criminal Procedure Code (CrPC) – Court to be open.
46 Section 146 Indian Evidence Act 1872 – Questions lawful in cross-examination.
47 Section 357C CrPC – Treatment of victims.
48 S. 357 CrPC – Order to pay compensation.
49 S. 357 A CrPC – Victim compensation scheme.
50 S. 164 A CrpC – Medical examination of the victim of rape.
51 Section 27 of POCSO Act, 2012: Medical examination of a child.
52 Woolmington v. D.P.P.[1935] AC 462 (HL).
53 Dr.(Mrs.) Shalini S. Phansalkar Joshi, "Refresher Course for POCSO Courts-STANDARD OF PROOF," in *National Judicial Academy*, n.d., available at https://nja.gov.in/Concluded_Programmes/2019-20/P-1196_PPTs/3.Standard%20of%20Proof%20under%20Posco%20Act%20latest.pdf (Retrieved July 30, 2023).
54 Sanjana Rebecca Samuel, "POCSO Provisions: Valid Exceptions." *Deccan Herald*, November 15, 2021, available at https://www.deccanherald.com/opinion/in-perspective/pocso-provisions-valid-exception-1051137.html (visited on July 30, 2023).
55 Ibid.
56 WP (C) No. 15564 of 2017 (U).
57 National Commission for Protection of Child Rights, available at https://ncpcr.gov.in/ (visited on July 30, 2023, 23:56).
58 Sec. 44 of the POCSO Act- Monitoring of implementation of Act and inquiring into any matter relating to any offence under this Act.

59 Research Programme entitled "Response to the Offence of Rape by the Criminal Justice System – An Empirical Study in the States of Odisha, Jharkhand and West Bengal," Funded by the Indian Council for Social Science Research, Grant No. F. No. Gen-35/2017-18/1CSSR/RP.

60 The Wire, "New Criminal Bills: Opposition Submits List of 16 Domain Experts to Parl Panel for Eliciting Views," available at https://thewire.in/politics/new-criminal-bills-opposition-submits-list-of-16-domain-experts-to-parl-panel-for-eliciting-views

2 Criminal justice process from the child victim's lens

Introduction

The Indian Constitution does not define the term child anywhere in its texts. The United Nations Convention on the Rights of the Child (UNCRC) 1989, under Article 1, defines a child as "a human being below the age of eighteen years unless, under the law applicable to the child, majority is attained earlier." Therefore, the legal description of the term "child" tends to depend on the context under which it is being used. The term child has been defined under numerous laws in India. The Indian Majority Act, 1875, states that the age of majority is 18 years.[1] A child (plural: children) is a human being between the stages of birth and puberty[2] or between the developmental period of infancy and puberty.[3] In India, a minor, also known as a person under the age of majority, is often referred to as a child under the legal definition of the term. A child is someone who is under the age of 14, according to the Child Labour (Prohibition and Regulations) Act of 1986.[4] On the other hand, according to the Prohibition of Child Marriage Act 2006, the definition in terms of age is conditionally dependent on their gender, i.e., for women it is 18 years of age and for men it is 21 years of age.[5] Under Juvenile Justice (Care and Protection) Act 2000, a Juvenile or a child means an individual who has not finished eighteen years of age.[6] The Protection of Children against Sexual Offences Act 2012 (POCSO) defines a child as a person below the age of eighteen years.[7] Therefore, except for the Child Labour (Prohibition and Regulations) Act 1986, it may be observed that under most of the laws in India there is uniformity on the statutory age of a child being 18 years.

The United Nations Declaration of Basic Principles of Justice for Victims of Crime and Abuse of Power, which was approved on November 29, 1985, by the United Nations General Assembly,[8] defines victims as persons who have suffered harm, be it physical, mental, emotional or economic through acts or omissions that are in violation of criminal laws operative within member States. Under the aforementioned Declaration, a person may be regarded as a victim regardless of whether the offender is found, captured, charged, or found guilty and regardless of whether the offender and victim were related in any way.[9] The word "victim" is also believed to refer to those who have

DOI: 10.4324/9781003345244-2

experienced injury as a result of stepping in to help distressed victims or avoid victimization as well as the direct victim's close relatives or dependents. The Declaration also specifies that all people should be subject to its rules without regard to their race, colour, sex, age, language, religion, nationality, or other characteristics, and it identifies four key rights for crime victims, including:

1. *Right to access to justice and fair treatment* – Victims should be treated with kindness and respect for their inherent worth as people. According to the law, individuals have a right to speedy justice for the harm they have endured. Judicial and administrative institutions should be developed and improved as necessary to ensure that the victims have access to quick and equitable ways to get justice. The victims must be informed of their rights to restitution through different channels. According to the UN Declaration, the following actions should be taken to help guarantee that legal and administrative procedures are responsive to victims' needs:
    (a) Keeping the victims updated about the duration and progress of the proceedings as well as the outcome of their cases and the scope of their role, particularly in cases of serious offences.
    (b) Upholding the respect for the criminal justice system of the state in question and without any prejudice to the accused, allowing the victims' opinions and concerns to be addressed.
    (c) Giving support to the victims during the proceeding of the case.
    (d) Acting to provide a safe environment to the victims as well as their families and the witness, while the case is in progress.
    (e) Resolving matters expeditiously while ensuring that the cases concerning the victims are carried out in accordance with the procedures of the Court.
    Where applicable, informal dispute resolution methods such as mediation, arbitration, etc. should be used to facilitate speedy justice to the victims.
2. *Right of restitution* – Provisions of reasonable and equitable compensation to the victims, their families, or dependents in appropriate cases by the perpetrators or other parties responsible for their acts should be made available to the victims. Making reparations for hurt or loss and covering medical expenses for the treatment of injuries due to victimization and entitlement to due rights all are included in the restitution process. In addition to fines that form part of the sentence, restitution should be considered as a potential alternative sentence in criminal proceedings. In case any state official or agent was responsible for any wrongdoing, then restitution to the victims of violations of the criminal law of that jurisdiction is on such public official or other agent acting officially or quasi-officially.
3. *Right to compensation:* The states ought to try to offer monetary compensation to those who have sustained significant physical harm or

mental or physical health impairments, as well as to their families, especially to the dependents of those who have passed away or have become physically or mentally unable as a result of serious crimes and are victimized. When payment from the offender or other sources is not entirely forthcoming, this is extremely crucial. The establishment of national funds for compensation to victims and strengthening and expansion of such funds should be encouraged. Other compensation funds may also be formed for this purpose when it is appropriate, especially in circumstances where the state is incapable of providing the required financial relief.

4. *Right to assistance*: The victims should get the requisite physical, psychological, social, and financial support through governmental, non-official, local, and indigenous channels. The presence of pertinent health, social, and other services should be made known to victims, and they should have simple access to them. Authorities in the sectors of law enforcement, justice, health, and social services should have the appropriate training in order to comprehend the requirements of victims and the best practices for efficient and fast assistance.

In the 154th Law Commission Report, the Commission spoke about the necessity of a victim-friendly approach for criminal justice administration and suggested that the needs of the victims of crime should receive urgent attention in the response to crime.[10] The Malimath Committee extensively discussed the involvement of crime victims at all phases of the criminal justice system in its 2003 Report on Reforms of Criminal Justice System. The Committee also gave the idea of expanding the concept of victim compensation some thought. The Malimath Committee Report's recommendations were implemented in subsequent Code of Criminal Procedure (CrPC) changes that expanded the role of crime victims.

In the United Nations Declaration of Basic Principles of Justice for Victims of Crime and Abuse of Power the expression 'victim' meant not only the person who has directly suffered the injury (physical, mental, emotional suffering or economic loss) but also included those people who have suffered harm in due course on account of the crime. Further recognition of victim of crime is independent of the perpetrator being identified, apprehended, prosecuted, or convicted. In India, Sec. 2(wa) of CrPC defines a 'victim' as a person who has suffered any loss or injury caused by reason of the act or omission for which the accused person has been charged and the expression 'victim' includes the victim's guardian or legal heir. In the case of *Ram Phal vs. State*,[11] the Delhi High Court tried to clarify the scope of the definition of 'victim' where the Court summarized that "victim under Section 2(wa) CrPC includes a person who has suffered harm caused to the mind." Further the Supreme Court in *Satya Pal Singh v. State of M. P*[12] held that *the father of the deceased woman has a right to prefer an appeal before the High Court (under proviso to Section 372 of Cr.P.C.), as a father can be read as a victim, having suffered loss due to the death of his daughter (as defined under Section 2(wa) of Cr.P.C).*

We have seen in Chapter 1 that the recommendations by the various committees for inculcation of pro-victim provisions in the criminal laws and the Criminal Law Amendment Act of 2013 and 2018 have introduced many victim-friendly laws especially for the victims of sexual offences. In the case of child victims who are females, such laws introduced in the CrPC will be applicable; however, when it comes to boys unless the POCSO Act contains the victim-friendly provisions, the benefit cannot be extended to such victims. This dichotomy can be cured only when there is parity in the POCSO Act with the provisions of the general criminal laws.

Impacts of the sexual offences on the victims

Victims of sexual assault or rape go through extreme trauma and hardships. And the response of survivors varies in different situations and at times the symptoms of a sexual assault or rape might be immediate or they can linger for a very long period. However, the effects of the crime of rape on a person's body, mind, and emotions may be summed up in Table 2.1.

Sexual abuse and its impact on the child victim

Children who are sexually abused may suffer severe and long-lasting effects.[13] It severely impacts their ability to trust adults, especially if the person was in a fiduciary capacity, someone they loved; someone who should have protected them but who abused them. The impact that sexual abuse has, varies from child to child. Children are remarkably resilient and brave in the face of abuse, but for many of them, the harm is severe and lasts for years, if not a lifetime.[14]

Medical, psychological, sexual, repetitive (self-)injury, and other issues were all shown to be strongly related to child sexual abuse in a thorough meta-review of problems reported by survivors.[15] The immediate physical effects of child sexual abuse include severe wounds and profuse bleeding in the kid's intimate areas, resulting in excruciating pain and physical trauma.[16] Other physical effects may range from bruising difficulty in walking, soreness, broken, or dislocated bones and sexually transmitted infections and diseases. There is also a danger of unwarranted pregnancies among adolescent girls subjected to such abuse.

Sexual abuse of children can also have devastating, long-term repercussions. A child is known to suffer significant long-term damage to mental and emotional health when sexually abused. A victim's relationships, physical

Table 2.1 Physical, mental and emotional effects on victims[a]

Physical effects	Mental effects	Emotional effects
• Bruising (in cases where the victim resisted) • Loss of blood (vaginal or anal) • Finding difficult to walk • Soreness of the body • Broken including dislocated bones • Sexually transmitted diseases • Pregnancy	• Post traumatic stress disorder (PTSD), which includes nightmares, anxiety attacks, and racing thoughts • Depression, which includes feelings of melancholy or hopelessness, uncontrolled sobbing, fluctuations in weight, lethargy, or lack of interest in activities enjoyed earlier • Suicidal thoughts • Dissociation, leading to a lack of concentration on work or study and apathy towards ordinary interactions	• Trust issues • Sense of anger and self-blame • Feelings of shock or numbness, or loss of control or disoriented or helplessness or fear • Sensation of vulnerability • Feeling that these emotions are making him/her a weak person

[a] P.A. Resick, "The Psychological Impact of Rape." *Journal of Interpersonal Violence*, 8, no. 2 (1993): 223–255. https://doi.org/10.1177/088626093008002005

health, academic performance, ability to find a job, and overall quality of life may all be negatively impacted by these impacts, which may cascade. The abuse of a child is not only the violation of the physic but it is the violation of the innocence and purity of childhood of the child. It affects the entire psychology of the child and puts the child into a deep emotional crisis. Just like the effects of sexual abuse on a major woman, a victim of child sexual abuse may experience similar effects.[17] The child victim may also experience certain mental distress like PTSD, including hallucinations and nightmares of the traumatic experience, etc.[18] The psychological effects of the crime can include trust issues, feeling of fear, disorientation and vulnerability, blame and rage, numbness, helplessness, shock, loss of control, and also self-blame or guilt for "allowing" the crime to happen and allowing the belief that she is weak for having such reactions.[19]

Primary victimization, secondary victimization, and revictimization

The act of being victimized or turning into a victim is called victimization. The primary or direct victims of an act of harm have experienced physical violence, sexual assault, or other types of prolonged abuse. Following their victimization, their experiences might take on a variety of various forms. After being hurt, primary victims may experience physical, emotional, and financial suffering.

A secondary victim is a subcategory of the overarching indirect victim label.[20] Secondary victims may be such individuals who witness attacks on the victims or people who experience first-hand testimony of victims' experiences.[21] These people might be the family, friends, neighbours, or any passer-by. Secondary victims who witness a violent crime may suffer psychological trauma of their own as a result. A further type of secondary victimization, commonly referred to as post-crime victimization or double victimization, concerns subsequent victimization to the first victimization,[22] which is common in the case of sexual abuse victims. Inappropriate post-assault actions or language by medical personnel, the police, or other organizations with whom the victim interacts, for instance, may worsen the victim's suffering.

Sexual offences are particularly stigmatizing in societies where there are rigid taboos and sexual norms. And someone who has been raped, particularly if they were virgins before, may be perceived by society as being "damaged."[23] In these societies, victims could experience ostracization, be shunned by peer groups, be forbidden from getting married, or, if they're already married, get divorced. The victim of a sexual assault, abuse, or rape who experiences further trauma as a result of the responses of the criminal justice system is an example of secondary victimization. In circumstances of statutory rape, acquaintance rape, and drug-facilitated rape the chances of secondary victimization are high.

Studies reveal that "revictimization" describes a trend in which a person who has experienced abuse or a crime has a statistically increased likelihood of being victimized again, either soon after or, in the instance of childhood abuse, much later in adulthood.[24] Particularly noticeable in instances of sexual abuse is the latter tendency. Despite the near impossibility of obtaining an exact percentage, samples from numerous studies indicate that the rate of revictimization for those with histories of sexual assault is very high.[25] The causes of revictimization differ depending on the type of occurrence, and some processes are unclear. In the near term, risk factors that were previously present and that were not altered or reduced after the initial victimization sometimes lead to revictimization; in some cases, the victim is powerless to influence these variables. These risk factors include things like working or living in unsafe regions, having a troubled family, being violent, using drugs or alcohol, and being unemployed.[26]

It is extremely difficult to prevent adult victims of sexual assault from becoming victims again. There are several theories as to how this operates. Some scientists promote a maladaptive kind of learning, where the initial abuse instills wrong attitudes and behaviours that persist throughout adulthood. Because the victim has grown to accept abusive behaviour as "normal" and has learned to expect it from others in the context of partnerships, they may unknowingly seek out violent partners or cling to abusive relationships. A different theory makes use of the idea of learned helplessness. As far as children victims are concerned, especially when the abuse is perpetrated by a caregiver, they are placed in situations from which they have little to no chance of escaping. According to one idea, when faced with a situation where they cannot escape or defend themselves, their only alternative is to freeze, which is a by-product of pretending to be dead.[27] Many a times children continue to tolerate the sexual abuse without resistance or complaint as they devise "avoidance coping," which is closely associated with anxiety and depression and includes cognitive and behavioural implications targeted towards ignoring, rejecting, reducing, or other ways to avoid dealing with unpleasant demands.[28]

Phenomenon of shaming and victim blaming

Victim blaming is the custom of assigning the victim of a crime or other unfair act some or all of the guilt for the harm that was done to them. The term "blaming the victim" was first used by psychologist William Ryan in his 1971 in his book with the same title.[29] Ryan described *victim blaming* as an ideology that is used against black people in the United States to justify racism and social injustice. The repeated traumatization of a victim of sexual abuse, malpractice, or rape as a result of the reactions of other people or institutions by shaming results in secondary victimization. Examples of secondary victimization include victim blaming, doubting the victim's account, downplaying the severity of the assault, unsuitable post-assault care provided by medical professionals or other organizations, and forcing the victim to retell her story in front of various criminal justice system stakeholders.[30]

Victim blaming as a phenomenon has been prevalent in India since ancient times. Brihaspati, a sage from an ancient India in his treaties (Brihaspati (Nitisara) Samhita), have mentioned that if the rapist is of a low varna then the raped women shall have the same fate as her rapist, that is death.[31] Parashar, another sage who is credited with writing the first Purana (Vishnu Purana) in an attempt to make Brihaspati's laws more humane, suggested that a raped woman may return to normalcy when she is *sanctified* by her menstrual cycle after taking a pledge of asceticism. These ancient scriptures have success-fully indoctrinated the society to assume that the women should behave in a predetermined manner that is in harmony with the social dictum.[32] These statements make it quite evident that from the ancient time, the phenomenon of shaming has been associated with the rape victim rather than the rapist. Due to rape myths, sexual assault victims are stigmatized. In patrilineal societies with strict taboos on sex and sexuality and strong conventions and traditions, a female rape victim is particularly stigmatized.

Age of consent of the victim

The age of consent recognized in law for engaging in sexual activity before the POCSO Act was restricted only to girls, under IPC 1860. This age was initially fixed at 10 years, raised to 12 years in 1891, then to 14 years in 1925, and finally to 16 years in 1940. It continued to be at 16 till the Criminal Law (Amendment) Act, 2013 was enacted,[33] after the nationwide public outrage in the wake of the infamous Delhi gang rape case that took place on December 16, 2012, in New Delhi.[34] The age of consent was made as 18 years for both girls and boys under the POCSO Act, 2012, making it gender neutral. According to the IPC, 1860, Section 375, "any man having intercourse with a female below the age of 16, irrespective of her consent, was considered as rape, with the exemption for a married man having intercourse with his wife above 15 years of age,"[35] although the age of consent by girls for sexual intercourse was 18 years under POCSO Act. This difference in the age of consent for boys and girls was made uniform by the Supreme Court in *Independent Thought* v. *Union of India*[36] at the age of 18.

One problem associated with the age of consent is due to child marriages which is a reality in India (although voidable if either of the parties, petition to the District Court before or two years after attaining the statutory age of marriage, except for the State of Karnataka that declares the practice of child marriages voidable forever[37]). This consequently created an unforeseen situ-ation, where such couples involving child marriage gone for medical check-up for pregnancy made the doctors fulfilling their mandatory responsibility of reporting any sexual activity with a child to competent authorities. This resulted in the arrest of young husbands leaving their pregnant wives and children in economic and emotional distress.

Another problem caused by POCSO Act 2012 is in cases involv-ing romantic relations among young people.[38] These love cases may be due to consensual sexual intercourse between two adolescent children or between one adolescent child and another young adult. In the former case, as a matter of practice the boys end up being arrested and produced before the Juvenile Justice Board on the complaint usually filed by the parents of the girl and the girl is presented as a victim before the Child Welfare Committee.[39] This practice is not in consonance with the POCSO Act as the offences under this Act are gender neutral and the offence may be committed by a person of any sex on another person of any sex. Hence, in all such cases where the children themselves admit of a consensual relationship, both of them should be treated in the same manner as victims.[40] In cases where one of them is an adolescent and the other a young adult, it cannot be ignored that there may be a component of emotional manipulation by the older partner (offender) to the victim, especially when the person stands in the position of trust.[41]

Intersection of the child victim of sexual offences with the criminal justice system

In the case of *Delhi Domestic Working Women's Forum v. Union of India*,[42] the Supreme Court pointed out the defects of the existing Criminal Justice System in handling a victim of sexual offence viz.,

> rough treatment and inadequate attention are given to complaints. More often than not, the cops humiliate the victims. Rape cases have always been distressing for the victims. Giving testimony in court has been a damaging and bad experience. The victims frequently claim that they thought the experience was worse than the actual rape. Without a question, the court processes made the psychological anguish they had already experienced as a result of the rape itself worse and longer.[43]

In the following section, we will see how the child victim of sexual abuse interacts through the various stages of the criminal justice process.

Victim as the reporter of the offence

The POCSO Act under Section 19 prescribes the general procedure for the reporting of the offences and recording by the police of the child victim. It states that

> where the police are satisfied that the child victim needs care and protection, they shall make immediate arrangements for admitting the child into shelter home or to the nearest hospital within twenty-four hours of the report and also record their reasons in writing

(Sec. 19(5)).

Also, the police have to keep the Child Welfare Committee (CWC) and the Special Court as designated under the POCSO Act and in case no Special Courts have been designated, then the Court of Sessions should be intimated (Sec. 19(6)). It is also provided that no person reporting the offence shall incur any civil or criminal liability for informing in good faith under Sec. 19(7). The aspect of mandatory reporting has been introduced in the POCSO Act where failure to report such incidents in spite of having the knowledge may invite penal consequences. This aspect has been discussed in detail in the subsequent chapter on investigation.

Where the information of commission or attempt of rape[44] is given by a girl, then that has to be recorded by a woman police officer of the police station. If such a woman is disabled (temporarily/permanently/physically/mentally), then the recording of such statement by a police officer should be conducted at the residence of the victim or at an appropriate place of her choice, also ensuring the presence of the interpreter or the special educator. The recording of such information shall be videotaped too. Under Section 24 of the POCSO Act, the child's statement should be recorded at the residence of the victim or at any place of convenience and most likely by a woman officer not below the rank of a Sub-Inspector. This provision mandates certain obligations on the police viz. the officer to not be in uniform, while probing the child, never the child should come in contact with the abuser; no child shall be kept in the police station after evening for any purpose, and finally, maintaining the anonymity of the child from the media unless otherwise stated by the Court.

The victim's contacts with the police just after the incident indicate a lot about how the criminal justice system will treat the victims of that crime.[45] The patriarchal mentality of Indian police personnel contributes to their victim-precipitation strategy. The reporting officer questions the victims or their families aggressively when they contact the police, which discourages the victim from pursuing her case.[46] Studies show that victims of sexual assault were more adversely affected by the criminal justice system's handling of them than were victims of non-sexual offences.[47] According to the available research, one of the main causes of the underreporting of occurrences of sexual assault is the fear of being shamed by the involved stakeholders.[48]

Case study

Chapter VI of the POCSO Act 2012 provides the procedures of recording of statement of the victim by the police at the residence or any new place of convenience of the victim. From the responses of the police in the states of West Bengal (WB), Jharkhand (JH), and Odisha (OD), the authors tried to assess the mindset of the police while handling rape and victims of child sexual abuse under the POCSO Act. However, it was stated by the majority of the police stations that the convenience of the victim is given the utmost importance while recording the statement of the victim after they have reported the offence. However, from the responses of the police interviewed in OD (97%) and WB (85%), the police admitted to having recorded such statement at the police station. The obligation on the police officer regarding the presence of the guardian and the restriction of wearing uniform during recording the statement of the child was being mostly said to be complied with.

The data collection revealed that there were numerous police stations in the three states which functioned without any woman police officer. The Investigating Officers (IOs) further admitted that in such circumstances, a requisition is sent to the nearest police station for a woman officer. And such a woman officer records the statement of the child victim and proceeds ahead with the investigation as required by the law.

POCSO e-Box for children[49]

The National Commission for Protection of Child Rights' (NCPCR) webpage has the POCSO e-Box, an online complaint box for reporting child sexual abuse. This programme intends to make it easier for kids to report such offences to the Commission. According to the POCSO Act of 2012, the online complaint management system makes it simple to report violations and take prompt action against violators. The E-Box is very easy to use and will aid in protecting the complainant's confidentially. It represents a paradigm change since a child is no longer reliant on an adult to report abuse. All parent–teacher resource guides highly recommend and explain the E-Box and government child care hotline phone numbers like 1098 act as a safety net.

How it works?

The user just has to simply push a button named POSCO e-Box available at the link in the webpage of National Commission for Protection of Child Rights (NCPCR) website. The POCSO e-box of NCPCR accepts reports from young victims of cybercrime. In light of the rising threat of online crimes aimed at children, NCPCR has expanded the scope of POCSO e-box to address online stalking, online bullying, morphing of image, and child pornography. On the Commission's website, www.ncpcr.gov.in, there is an e-box button that may be used to report cybercrimes by either the child victims themselves or their friends, parents, relatives, or guardians.

Victim in the investigation stage

Once the First Information is registered (First Information Report is commonly known as FIR), the police start the investigation. If the sexual assault victim is a girl the provisions of the CrPC will apply and if the victim is a *minor* (child below 18 years of age) whether girl or boy, the POCSO Act being the special law, will apply. Wherever there is any gap in the POCSO Act then the CRPC will apply. At the investigation stage, the victim's statement is recorded under Section 24 of the POCSO Act as the primary witness of the case by the police. The next significant step is the medical examination of the child victim according to Section 27 of the POCSO Act. According to Rule 6 of the POCSO Rules 2012,

> the officer upon receiving information under Section 19 of the Act that an offence has been committed, is obliged to arrange as soon as possible, but within 24 hours, for taking the victim-child to the nearest hospital or medical care centre for any emergency medical care.

The victim should be mandatorily sent to emergency medical care where an offence of penetrative sexual assault has been committed under Section 3 of the Act, aggravated penetrative sexual assault under Section 5, sexual assault under Section 7, or aggravated sexual assault under Section 9 of the Act. This is discussed in detail in the subsequent chapter on Investigation.

The Indira Gandhi Matritva Sahayog Yojana and the One-Stop Centre Scheme, popularly known as Sakhi, are both parts of the umbrella programme of the National Mission for Empowerment of Women, which was established on April 1, 2015.[50] The centrally supported programme was developed by the Ministry of Women and Child Development (MWCD). The MWCD wants to establish one-stop facilities all throughout the nation to provide comprehensive assistance to women and children and free them from the cycle of abuse, whether it occurs in public or private settings.

Regardless of their age, class, level of education, culture, etc., the One-Stop Centres (OSCs) support women and children who have experienced physical, emotional, psychological, or sexual abuse.[51] These Centres aid all women, regardless of caste, creed, marital status, religion, or sexual orientation, whose safety is threatened by the violence. The benefits of the programme are simply accessible to all age groups in difficult situations. Additionally, it offers them total support and recourse, enabling them to break free from the chains of pervasive violence and prejudice. One of the goals of the programme is to give the affected women urgent, emergency, and non-emergency help, including psychological counselling and legal advocacy.

The One-Stop Centre Scheme facilitates the victim with multiple services viz.:

- Emergency Response and Rescue Services: As soon as a woman discloses her problems, the OSC offers rescue and referral services. They cooperate with the National Health Mission's (NHM) 108 services and PCR vans to help the infected women go to a hospital or shelter house close by.
- Medical Assistance: According to the Ministry of Health and Family Welfare's recommendations, affected women receive medical assistance and exams.
- Psycho-Social/Support Counselling: The victim's self-confidence has been severely damaged by a traumatic event. In order to help the victim face the situation and seek redress, the one-stop centre plan also includes a trained therapist who will perform the counselling session.
- Legal Aid and Counselling: OSC also offers appointed solicitors or National/State/District Legal Service Authorities to assist a victim in pursuing justice.
- Video Conferencing Facility: OSC offers a video conferencing facility where the victimized woman or kid may also record her remarks in order to expedite the police and legal processes.

In the sample states where the research was conducted, the functionality of OSCs is questionable in West Bengal, as opposed to Jharkhand and Odisha. The s. 164A CrPC[52] clause, which was added in 2005, recognized the significance of the victim's permission, the need for an immediate medical assessment, and the procedure to be followed. Although there is no uniform process of collecting samples and reporting, this provision made the first attempt to standardize the system in rape cases. The legislation requires that the rape victim be examined within 24 hours of learning of the violation by a registered medical officer or practitioner (doctor) in the closest government institution, or, in the event that this doctor is not available, by any other registered doctor with the woman's agreement. This is one of the most important steps, since substantial evidence is expected from such examination and also medically treating the victim during the course of such examination.

Case study

According to the data gathered, all of the police in OD, JH, and 97% of the police in WB, have confirmed that the victims are sent for medical examinations within 24 hours of receiving the report.

Only 1% of IOs in WB did not react when asked about the victim's medical evaluation. The police may not like to admit it, but one explanation for such missing data might be that these regulations are not being followed. It was acknowledged that delays can result from the lack of female doctors in the hospitals.

Victim as a witness during trial

The Witness Protection Scheme which was approved on December 5, 2018, by the Apex Court 2018 aimed at enabling the witnesses to depose fearlessly and truthfully. Although the scheme is still in the Parliament and yet to be passed, the Supreme Court has ordered that it be put into effect right away in every state and become the rule of law. This plan aims to provide witnesses with proper and sufficient protection. The purpose of this programme is to help the endangered and vulnerable witnesses and to inspire confidence in their ability to testify in court. In-camera trials, close physical protection, anonymized testimony, and references to witnesses in the records are just a few of the facilities that work to better safeguard witnesses. In-camera trials in front of parents or any other person the kid has confidence in are required by Section 37 of the POCSO Act. Section 38 speaks of the appointment of translators or interpreters wherever necessary.

Section 118 of the Indian Evidence Act of 1872 states that anyone can testify during a trial unless they are unable to comprehend and respond to the questions that are posed to them. In *Suresh v. State of U.P.*[53] according to the Supreme Court, a 5-year-old girl's evidence is admissible since she was able to comprehend and understand the question. The court further stated that a child's testimony is acceptable if they can comprehend and understand the inquiry. In the case of *Suryanarayan v. State of Karnataka*,[54] the confirmation of the testimony, according to the Supreme Court, is only a recommendation to proceed cautiously rather than a requirement. If the witness statement has no significant inconsistencies that are afterwards accepted and cannot be used as justification to throw out the evidence. The Courts may only rely on that witness' testimony if they are certain that no tutoring occurred and the youngster did not confuse reality with fantasy.

The Supreme Court of India in *Smruti Tukaram Badade v. State of Maharashtra & Anr.*[55] issued directions for the immediate establishment of at least two vulnerable witness deposition centres under every High Court's jurisdiction. It has become more important to safeguard vulnerable witnesses in criminal cases. Children, rape survivors, sexual abuse victims, and others frequently find the courtroom situation distressing. Even if not physically, they are always in danger emotionally. Due to the mental trauma faced by the victims as a result of other institutions or people after the crime has been committed, especially in situations of sexual abuse, this results in secondary victimization of vulnerable witnesses.

Section 26 of the POCSO Act speaks of the additional procedures regarding the recording of the statement of the child by the Magistrate. The presence of parents during the recording of the statement of the child victim has to be ensured by the Magistrate and the assistance of the interpreter has to be taken in times of need and wherever possible, the recording of the statement has to be recorded through audio–video means. Further Chapter VIII of the POCSO Act also deals with procedures and powers of Special Courts while recording of evidence of the child victim. Section 33 provides that, firstly

> the Special Court can take cognizance of any offence under this Act without the accused being committed to it for trial (Section 33(1)). Secondly, special care must be taken by the courts to ensure that during examination of the child during cross-examination, examination-in-chief or re-examination, the questions are to be put to the child via the Court (Section 33(2)); thirdly, frequent breaks are to be allowed during trial to the child when necessary (Sec. 33(3)); fourthly, the child is not repeatedly called to the court to testify (Sec. 33(5)). And finally, aggressive questioning or character assassination of the child shall not be allowed and the court must make sure that the dignity of the child is maintained at all times during the trial (Sec. 33(6)).

Case study

From the data collected from the stakeholders, the trial court Judges responded that in almost all cases they prefer to have an in-camera trial so as to make the victim of child sexual abuse feel comfortable before deposing in the court. For most of the Courts, the Judges responded to the fact the child is called only once to the Court to testify. This is done to ensure that the child victim is not subject to secondary victimization because of the repeated deposition in the Court. Breaks are also being allowed to the child victim whenever necessary (50% in OD, 54% in WB, and 80% in JH).

Victim's anonymity clause

Because sexual offences are serious in nature and have societal repercussions, it is the responsibility of the state as well as people to take all necessary steps to ensure that an innocent victim may live a dignified life after the traumatic experience. Sexual offence victims are often mocked, ridiculed, and decried when they go out in the public.[56] Especially in rural areas, women (including girl child) who have been raped are looked at with disdain, and their demeanour, however normal, is seen as morally reprehensible and is unfairly associated with the rape.[57] While family prevents them from voicing their opinions or from taking personal decisions, old friends often avoid and refuse to see them.[58] While older women are out casted in reprehensible ways, young girls who have been raped are considered bad examples and thus expelled from schools. In order to neutralize the effect of stigma and shame attached to a victim of sexual assault, the victim anonymity clause was introduced in the IPC under Section 228A.

The IPC under Section 228A[59] forbids and makes it illegal to print or distribute any information relating to the identity of a rape victim. However, in *Bhupinder Sharma v. State of Himachal Pradesh*,[60] when Section 228A was specifically mentioned, the Supreme Court ruled that this provision does not apply to printing or publishing Supreme Court or High Court judgements. Nevertheless, keeping in mind the goal of preventing social stigma or ostracization of the victim of a sexual offence, the court also observed that it is appropriate to omit the victim's name from the judgements. Again, in *Commissioner, Trade Tax, Uttar Pradesh v. M/S Malkhan S. Subhash Chandra*,[61] the Courts stressed on the need to amend the cause titles disclosing the victim's names in sexual assault cases. In *Nipun Saxena v. Union of India*,[62] it was decided that the victim's anonymity had to be preserved as much as possible during the investigation, the trial, and even after the verdict was given. In *State of Punjab v. Gurmit Singh*,[63] it further issued a directive not to disobey the requirements of this clause and to hold the rape case trials in-camera (i.e., not open to the public) that would help the victim feel a little more at ease and respond to the questions more readily. As a result, it is anticipated that the victim's testimony will be of higher quality since she will not be as reluctant to testify in open court in front of the public. Additionally, it was mandated that, to the extent practical and possible, a female judge presided over the trial in certain circumstances so that the victim would have enough time to present her side of the story and provide support. However, these provisions have been specifically designed for a female victim to deal with offences of rape under the IPC. Statistics show that in 99% of POCSO cases,[64] the victims are females; therefore, these provisions are equally applicable to girl child victims of sexual offences.

The media must take steps in favour of children while reporting any matter connected to sexual crimes against any child. This is provided under Section 23 of the POCSO Act[65] that prohibits giving of any statement on any child through any form of media or studio or photographic facilities without having complete and authentic information, as it may lead to shaming the child by infringing upon his privacy. There is also a bar on reporting in any media, disclosing the name or any other details regarding the identity of the child.

However, a disclosure is permissible by the Special Court if such disclosure is shown to be in the interest of the child. Additionally, the publisher and owner of the media, studio, or photography facilities will be jointly and severally accountable for any act of his employee and the Court must impose a sentence of not less than six months and up to one year in jail, as well as a fine, or a combination of the two, in the event that the law is broken. The Special Court must make sure that the child's identity is never revealed during an inquiry or trial, according to Section 33(7) of the Act.[66]

Victim-friendly steps during the process of Criminal Justice administration

It is critical to recognize that victims of rape experience post traumatic repercussions that range from physical to psychological illnesses, necessitating a greater level of medical attention.[67] After the Delhi gang rape case, the Verma Committee was established. Based on its recommendations, the rape laws were revised in 2013. Some of the recommendations stated that the police should treat rape victims with compassion and devoid of rape myths, counsel the victim, and if required also refer the victim for psychological counselling if she was in trauma. In addition, the states were required to establish receiving centres in line with rape crisis centres to offer the victim one-stop rehabilitation.[68] Unavailability of post traumatic counselling poses a threat to the repairment of the victim.[69]

The POCSO Act provides that the Special Court shall create an atmosphere conducive to the child by firstly ensuring the presence of a family member, a friend, or a guardian to be present in the court (Section 33(4)); secondly, the identity of the child should not be revealed at any time during investigation or trial (Section 33(7)); thirdly, the child while giving her testimony is not exposed in any way to the accused, though the accused should be able to hear what the child is testifying and also be able to communicate with his counsel (Section 36). The purpose of all these provisions is to provide a child-friendly environment and during trial for the child victim who is the most important witness. Also, due to the stigma attached with the crime the child-friendly provisions also attempt to ensure participation and cooperation of the child during prosecution and trial.

Case study

The data collected from the IOs replicate the reality of the attitudes of the police towards the victims of child sexual abuse in the sample states where the research was conducted. It demonstrates the disparity in police mentalities between JH and WB, where the majority held the opposite opinion, and OD, where the popular perception was that police dealt with rape cases differently (and with compassion). Since the first impression has an impact on future interaction between the victim, the prosecution, and the judge, it is crucial for the police to show empathy for the victim[70] According to the data collected only in WB (87%) are victims directed for psychological treatment, as opposed to OD or JH where this is not the case.

According to Section 357C of the CrPC, all hospitals, whether public or private, are required to offer urgent first aid or medical care to victims of crimes against women (including rape) at no expense to them and to thereafter notify the police right once. It is to be considered that immediate first aid shall also include stabilizing the victim psychologically for her restoration. As a matter of practice, the police must take care of such victims if they need immediate medical attention because, in the majority of cases, the victims seek the police before going to the hospital. 3% of the IOs in WB did not react to the question on approaching her with sensitivity. In response to the questions about providing the victim with post traumatic counselling, reasons for not providing the victim with post traumatic counselling were because there are no rape crisis centres in the district, and reasons for not providing the victim with post traumatic counselling because there are no directions towards the same, 1% of the respondents did not respond. These IOs' lack of reactions demonstrates that they do not share the WB's victim-friendly mentality. Similar to this, JH reported 2% missing data for several of the questions about the victim being counselled by the police, the victim being referred for psychiatric therapy, and the victim's family being counselled to assist her. Such missing information can be a sign of the police's lack of interest in helping the victim.

Compensation to the victim

Compensation to a victim of sexual offence is an important aspect of the restoration and restoration, specially in a civilization where such victims are treated worse than the perpetrator. However, monetary compensation may not restore the victim emotionally, but it definitely allows the victim to use the money for her physical and mental rehabilitation. Section 357 CrPC aims at providing compensation to the victims of crime on account of the sentenced person from the fine amount or compensation paid by the offender in case fine does not form part of the punishment.[71] Section 357 was incomplete in itself as it did not provide for all the victims of the crime where the trial cannot be concluded, for instance, where the accused has died or escaped or discharged or acquitted due to deficient evidence. In order to close this gap, the legislature added Section 357A, which made the state responsible for compensating the victim or any dependents who suffered as a result of the crime.[72] Under Section 357 of the Code of Criminal Procedure, there was no obligation on the State to compensate the victim even when the accused was not identified, or discharged or acquitted, which was a major flaw. However, Section 357A was a constructive measure to address the victims' problems. According to this provision, the State is responsible for compensating the victim or his or her dependents who have suffered as a result of the crime where the offender cannot be found, cannot be found guilty, or the compensation provided by the offender under Section 357 CrPC is insufficient. Every State Government is required by Section 357A to create a Victim Compensation Scheme in collaboration with the Central Government.[73] The victim of a crime or his or her dependents will be able to make a claim through this programme for compensation for their loss or harm. The State is required to establish and manage a fund for paying out such compensation. There are two ways that a victim might profit from victim compensation. First, the District Legal Service Authority (DLSA) or the State Legal Service Authority (SLSA) may be recommended for compensation by the court considering the victim's case. Then, in accordance with the plan in place in their state, the authorities will compensate the sufferer. Second, Section 357(4) permits the victim to apply directly to the DLSA or the SLSA for compensation. Since the 2008 amendment, almost every state has developed its own victim compensation programme with minimum and maximum levels of compensation for offences given provided in the scheme.

The SLSA and DLSA must receive both a physical copy and an electronic copy of the FIR in order for the police to report the offences covered by this scheme. Additionally, it enables SLSA/DLSA to voluntarily launch fact-finding investigations in order to provide victims with interim compensation. Additionally, it has provisions for immediate compensation in worthy circumstances, which may be in the amount of Rs. 5,000–10,000. According to the Central Victim Compensation Fund Scheme Guidelines, it has further increased the minimum amount of compensation for rape cases to Rs. 4 lakhs and 5 lakhs for gang rape.[74] The programme represents a crucial turning point in the social growth and rehabilitation of female victims. However, the programme has just recently been implemented; therefore, we have not yet evaluated its effects.

Compensation for child victim under POCSO Act and Rules

According to Sec. 33(8) of the POCSO Act, the Special Courts have the authority to direct payment of any compensation that may be prescribed to the child for bodily or mental stress inflicted or for prompt rehabilitation in addition to punishment. In *Nipun Saxena v. Union of India*,[75] the Supreme Court ordered the National Legal Services Authority (NALSA) to create the Model Rules for Victim Compensation for Sexual Offences and Acid Attacks in order to create parity in the victim compensation programmes of various states and UTs. Thus, a new chapter titled Compensation Scheme for Women Victims/Survivors of Sexual Assault/Other Crimes was added. However, the POCSO Act, which has its own system and procedures for compensating young victims of sexual abuse, is not covered by this chapter. It further clarifies that under sec. 33(8) of the POCSO Act and Rule 7 of the POCSO Rules (now Rule 9 as per updated rules 2020), only the learned Special Courts are authorized to handle compensation-related matters. However, compensation may be provided under the State Victim Compensation Scheme if the child is the victim of an incident that is not a sexual offence as defined by the POCSO Act.

Accordingly, Rule 9(1) of the POCSO Rules 2020, the court may also grant interim compensation to satisfy immediate needs, provide relief, or facilitate rehabilitation at any point following the registration of the FIR. Interim compensation is to be deducted from the final compensation awarded in the appropriate cases. In addition, according to Rule 9(2)

> the court can recommend the award of compensation whether the accused is found guilty, even acquitted or discharged, or remains untraced or unknown, if the court determines that the victim has suffered loss or injury as a result of the offence.

The Special Court is allowed to direct the payment of compensation to the victims under Rule 9(3) of the POCSO Rules 2020.

In Mother Minor Victim No. 1 & 2 v. State and others,[76] the Delhi High Court held that,

> *It is well settled that every statutory power is also coupled with the duty to exercise it. In view of the express provisions of Section 33(8) of the POCSO Act and Rule 7 of the said Rules (Rule 9 of the Protection of Children from Sexual Offences Rules, 2020 as is currently in force), the duty to award compensation in appropriate cases has been conferred on the Special Court and therefore, it is incumbent on the Special Court to pass necessary orders for compensation/interim compensation in appropriate cases. It is not open for the Special Court to delegate the said power and direct the concerned Legal Services Authority to examine any claim for compensation payable to a minor victim of an offence punishable under the POCSO Act.* (emphasis original)

However, as held by the Delhi High Court in MST. X (THROUGH MOTHER AND NATURAL GUARDIAN) Vs STATE & ORS[77] when an application for compensation comes in front of the Court, the court may in its discretion, do any one of three things:

> firstly, if the application is for interim compensation, the court may order the payment of interim compensation to the victim; secondly, if the application is for compensation, the court may recommend the award of compensation without stating the amount to be paid, leaving it to the concerned legal service authority to quantify it; or thirdly, if the application is for compensation, the court may recommend the award of compensation without specifying the amount to be paid.

Case study

According to the responses of the Judges in the three states, most of the Judges in most of the cases have recommended the matter to the concerned Legal Services Authority for the grant of compensation. It was stated that in cases that lacked merits, compensation was not granted. The basis for deciding the quantum of compensation was the nature and extent of the injury to the victim, nature of the offence, and the paying capacity of the offender.

Best practices from across the globe

The policies for improving investigations, trial, and generally responding to sexual offences against children endorsed by a substantial number of policy-makers and professionals may be considered as the "best practice towards victims of Child Sexual Abuse." This segment will cover some of the best practices being followed across the world and in India in an attempt to improve the investigations for sexual offences against children.

Child abuse services team, Orange County, California (CAST)

What is CAST?

CAST was created in 1989 with the purpose of reducing the trauma for child victims of abuse during the process of investigation. The participants of CAST include child advocates, Deputy District Attorneys, police, doctors, social workers, therapists, and Victim Witness Specialists in a multi-discipline public–private cooperation. Due to its child friendly approach, it is considered to be suitable for handling child abuse investigations, and it is a nationally recognized leader and role model as a member of the National Children's Alliance. It aims to reduce the trauma for victims of child abuse through the following ways:

- Minimizing the number of sessions with the child
- Limiting investigations through the child
- Providing a child advocacy on-site, to the victim and family
- Providing help for crisis intervention and referrals for therapy
- Conducting the interview and examination at a single, non-threatening child-friendly site
- Protecting the victim
- Providing access to the Victim/Witness Assistance Program

Who can bring a child to CAST?

Only a child protective agency can arrange for children to come to CAST. The Child Abuse Registry or the Law enforcement agency in the city or the area in which the crime may have occurred can be contacted for taking the child victim to CAST. It started as a single-site multidisciplinary team programme for looking into cases of child sexual abuse. Since this one-stop strategy was so effective, it was expanded to cover all types of child abuse in 1999. Children who have experienced severe physical and emotional abuse as well as those who have seen crimes like domestic violence, kidnapping, and murder are now served by CAST. Social services, police enforcement, deputy district attorneys, healthcare professionals, and therapists may now work together on investigations thanks to CAST's integrated on-site services. As a result, investigations are finished more quickly, completely, and consistently. During the child abuse inquiry, this is advantageous to the family as well as the kid.

The child-focused, kid-friendly environment at CAST helps these kids recover from their trauma in a more profound way. They can play peacefully at CAST, while the non-offending parents receive prompt assistance from trained personnel and volunteers. The youngsters are comforted by community gifts of toys, games, plush animals, snacks, lunches, and crafts.

Child Abuse Prevention and Treatment Act (CAPTA) (United States[78])

The United States has established comprehensive frameworks for child protection at both the federal and state levels. One of the key federal laws addressing child abuse, including sexual abuse, is the Child Abuse Prevention and Treatment Act (CAPTA). This law provides guidelines for developing and implementing child abuse prevention and intervention programmes by states.

Under CAPTA, states are required to have procedures in place for the reporting, investigation, and treatment of child abuse cases, including sexual

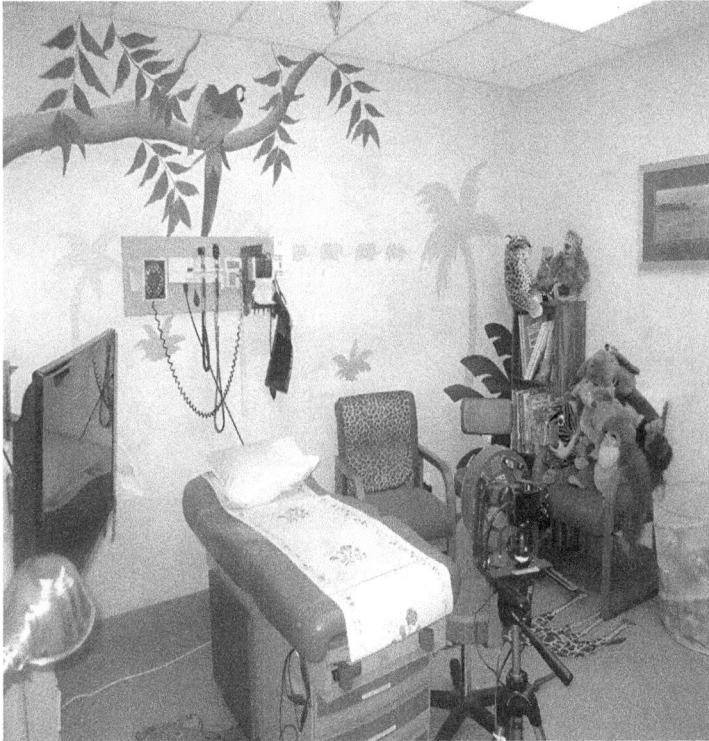

Figure 2.1 Medical emergency room at CAST, Orange County.

Picture taken by one of the authors, Prof. Paromita Chattoraj in November 2013 (Received the ICSSR grant in 2013–14 for data Collection in California, USA, for comparative research on Rape Investigation and Prosecution in India and USA.)

abuse. These procedures typically involve a collaborative approach among various agencies, such as child protective services, law enforcement, medical professionals, and mental health providers.

Additionally, each state in the United States has its own child protection laws and procedures that work in conjunction with CAPTA. These state laws may provide additional guidelines, definitions, and requirements specific to that jurisdiction. They outline the process for reporting suspected child abuse, the responsibilities of mandated reporters, the procedures for investigating allegations, and the provision of services and support to child victims.

Figure 2.2 Receiving room for sexually abused child, CAST, Orange County.
Ibid.

The state-level child protection systems often involve multidisciplinary teams and collaborations between agencies and professionals to ensure a coordinated response to child abuse cases. These systems aim to protect the child's well-being, provide appropriate interventions and treatment, and hold perpetrators accountable for their actions.

The National Society for the Prevention of Cruelty to Children (NSPCC) and the Child Exploitation and Online Protection (CEOP) Centre[79] (United Kingdom)

The United Kingdom has a well-developed child protection system in place, which includes guidelines and frameworks provided by organizations such as the NSPCC and the CEOP Centre. These organizations play a crucial role in raising awareness, providing support, and offering guidance on child protection issues, including sexual abuse.

In addition to these guidelines, the United Kingdom has specific legislation in place to address child abuse and sexual offences. The Children Act 1989 is a key piece of legislation setting out the obligations of local authorities and courts to safeguard and promote the welfare of children. It outlines the principles that guide decision-making in relation to child protection, including the need to prioritize the child's best interests.

The Sexual Offences Act 2003 is another important piece of legislation that specifically addresses sexual offences, including those committed against children. This act defines and criminalizes various forms of sexual abuse, provides provisions for the protection and support of victims, and establishes penalties for perpetrators. The UK's child protection system operates through multi-agency collaboration, involving various professionals and organizations working together to safeguard children and respond to instances of abuse. This collaborative approach includes social services, law enforcement agencies, healthcare professionals, educators, and other relevant stakeholders.

Furthermore, the UK government has implemented initiatives to tackle child sexual exploitation, online abuse, and grooming. The CEOP Centre, which is now part of the National Crime Agency (NCA), has the primary objective of combating child sexual exploitation and online child sexual abuse. They provide resources, training, and support to professionals and the public, working towards the prevention and detection of such offences.

The Swedish Social Services Act (Socialtjänstlagen)[80]

Sweden is recognized for its well-regarded child protection system, which places a strong emphasis on promoting the best interests of the child. The Swedish Social Services Act (Socialtjänstlagen) is a key piece of legislation that provides guidelines for the investigation and support of child victims of sexual abuse. The Swedish Social Services Act outlines the responsibilities and obligations of social services in protecting children and ensuring their well-being. The Act emphasizes on the principle that decisions and interventions should prioritize the best interests of the child. It sets the framework for the investigation of child abuse cases, including sexual abuse, and establishes procedures for assessing and providing support to child victims.

The act highlights the importance of collaboration among different agencies and professionals involved in child protection, such as social workers, police, healthcare providers, and educators. It promotes a multidisciplinary approach to ensure a comprehensive and coordinated response to cases of child abuse. In addition to the Swedish Social Services Act, Sweden has established various guidelines and resources to support professionals in their work with child victims of sexual abuse. For example, the National Board of Health and Welfare (Socialstyrelsen) has developed guidelines for child protection and forensic interviews with child victims, aiming to ensure a child-centred and sensitive approach during the investigative process.

Furthermore, organizations like BRIS (Children's Rights in Society) provide support and helpline services for children who have experienced abuse, including sexual abuse. These organizations play a vital role in raising aware-ness, providing information, and aiding child victims and their families.

Sweden's child protection system reflects a commitment to prioritizing the best interests of the child and ensuring their safety, well-being, and recov-ery from sexual abuse. The combination of legislation, guidelines, and sup-port services contributes to a comprehensive and child-centred approach to addressing child sexual abuse in Sweden.

Vertical prosecution system

There are two ways that prosecutors pursue criminal charges: vertically or horizontally. When each step of the procedure is handled by a separate pros-ecutor, a case is prosecuted horizontally. When a case is prosecuted verti-cally, victims can cooperate with the same prosecutor and investigator from the moment prospective charges are initially examined until the defendant is sentenced. It has been demonstrated that vertical prosecution increases con-viction rates, lessens victim trauma, and results in more consistent, suitable sentences. It is thus considered as a best practice.[81] Vertical prosecution can be traced back to 1979, when the Los Angeles District Attorney's Office estab-lished Operation Hardcore (now known as the Hardcore Gang Investigations Unit), a specialized prosecution unit devoted to violent gang crimes, with support from the federal government. Despite the fact that they were gang-related cases, prosecutors treated them vertically or continuously, and addi-tional investigation help (such as money for witness relocation) was given.[82] One method the legal system might assist crime victims is by designating one prosecutor to handle their case from the preliminary hearing through the tri-al's punishment phase, or whenever the victim is required to appear in court. Having one person in the process that the victim of a sexual crime thinks is on their side is crucial to helping them feel comfortable and like they have someone to talk to. They have a single person they can turn to for information and assistance, preventing the court process from becoming impersonal.[83] As a result, the prosecutor and victim develop deeper bonds in which the victim feels valued and involved and the prosecutor is certain that they are pursuing justice for both the victim and society as a whole. Victims should be more willing to testify if they feel empowered, a part of the process, and helping the prosecutor convict the criminal.[84]

In India there is a disconnect between the victim and the prosecutor. In fact, there is no statutory obligation on the prosecutor to take the victim into account or give him/her any hearing or notify the victim about the case pro-gress or outcome. As crimes are considered as an attack on the State, the prosecutor represents the state during a criminal trial and in the process the victims get indirectly represented. Although a proviso was added to Sec. 24(8) CrPC by the 2008 Criminal Law Amendment paving the way for the victim to engage an advocate of choice to assist the public prosecutor, however, such victim's counsel role is only secondary to the public prosecutor. Although the it is the choice of the victim's counsel to make up for any oversights or deficiencies in the prosecution case.[85] However, there is no occasion where the law provides for an interaction between the prosecutor and the victim, whether horizontally or vertically. This is more so because the Prosecutor in India is not involved in the investigation at all. The police officer (who should be a woman officer as mandated by Section 154 CrPC after the 2013 Criminal Law Amendment) responds to the victim as a first responder and records the information. Generally, the police officer who records the information may not be the one who investigates.[86] Therefore, during the investigation, when her statements are recorded (Section 161 CrPC), or he/she is taken for the medical examination (Section 164A CrPC), or when she is taken before a Magistrate for recording the statement on oath (Section 164 CrPC), there is no guarantee that she will be handled by the same police officer, thereby making the system predominantly horizontal.

International legal precedent also implies that courts are likely to favour an audio-visual recording of the witness's remarks.[87] Additionally, this lessens the likelihood of discrepancies between an individual's previous remarks and future court testimony.[88] In India the law permits audio-videographic recording while recording at the stage of FIR (u/s.154 CrPC), recording by the police (u/s.161 CrPC), of statement of the victim as a witness of crime and also at the time of recording of the statement of witness (child victim) by the Magistrate (u/s164 CrPC), the idea is to relieve the victim from repeating the traumatic account of the abuse, but our case study revealed that 77% of the policemen in the state of Odisha, 10% in Jharkhand, and 81% in West Bengal agreed to the fact that there are facilities for audio–video recording of the statement of the victim and that they do such recording of statements. But when the same question was asked to the Judges of the Special Courts regarding the admission of audio–video graphed statements recorded by the police for corroboration in during the trial, only 50% of the Judges in Odisha, 12.5% in West Bengal, and 30% in Jharkhand stated they allow such statements to be used for corroborating the case of the victim. This shows a disparity in the statements given and the actions done by the police. On the other hand, most of the Judges who stated in negative that they do not allow the audio–video recorded statement of the victim mentioned that in most of the cases the police never produces such recordings in front of the Judge to consider for the purposes of trial. This defeats the purpose of the law despite the idea being to protect the victim from repeating her account of the incident numerous times, he/she would be forced to do so on account of such non-compliances by the police.

Way forward for the victims

Many nations underwent significant transformation after the Declaration of Basic Principles of Justice for Victims of Crime and Abuse of Power was adopted. However, there is still a widespread absence of laws governing the support of crime victims. The absence of political will to take any action in this area may be one of the causes. The policymakers should be careful not to overlook any crucial elements while drafting measures to aid victims. This should include steps taken to ensure that the victim's privacy, dignity, or personal freedom is not violated in the pursuit of justice. The victim is at his own mercy once the investigation gets underway. Such a person is victimized not just by the accused's punishment but also by all the judgements and social exclusion he encounters. One of the primary reasons why people fail to disclose crimes, particularly those involving children, is sometimes attributed to societal pressure. When the case is being investigated and tried, precautions should be taken to ensure that the child victim is not regarded differently by society and institutional stakeholders like the police and courts. For this, it is crucial to conduct awareness-raising activities for kids, parents, and regular society members understanding the POCSO Act's provisions, in addition to passing laws prohibiting such crimes. It is because of which the POCSO Act provides for Section 43[89] of the Act which emphasizes on wide publicity and awareness building about this law. The National and/or State Commission of women has been vested with the responsibility of monitoring the implementation of the Act (Section 44 POCSO Act).[90] Overall, we can see how important a role the state plays in the Indian criminal justice system. However, it is crucial to give the victim a major role throughout the whole procedure and even after the proceedings are over in order to ensure that justice is effectively served.

Notes

1　Section 3 The Majority Act 1875– Age of majority of persons domiciled in India. https://archive.org/details/mosbysdictionary09edunse/page/344/mode/2up?q=345.
2　*Mosby's Dictionary of Medicine, Nursing & Health Professions* (St. Louis: Elsevier Health Sciences), 344. Accessed on July 7, 2023. Available at https://archive.org/ details/mosbysdictionary09edunse/page/344/mode/2up?q=345.
3　S.A. Rathus, "Childhood and Adolescence: Voyages in Development." *Cengage Learning* (2013): 48. ISBN 978-1-285-67759-0
4　Section 2(ii) – Definitions – Child Labour (Prohibition and Regulations) Act, 1986.
5　Section 2(a) – Definition – Prohibition of Child Marriage Act 2006. As per the PROHIBITION OF CHILD MARRIAGE (AMENDMENT) BILL, 2021 which is yet to be passed, the definition of child is proposed to be uniform for both the genders and says "child" means a male or female who has not completed twenty-one years of age.
6　Section 2(12) – Definitions – Juvenile Justice (Care and Protection) Act, 2000.
7　Section 2(d) – Definitions – Protection of Children against Sexual Offences Act 2012.
8　United Nations Declaration of Basic Principles of Justice for Victims of Crime and Abuse of Power adopted on November 29, 1985.
9　Dr. R.N. Mangoli and Nandini G. Devarmani, "Role of Victims in Criminal Justice System: A Critical Analysis from Indian Perspective." *SSRN Journal* (2014), available at https://www.ssrn.com/abstract=2814578 (visited on June 1, 2023).

10 K. Aggarwal, S. Dalwai, P. Galagali, D. Mishra, C. Prasad and A. Thadhani, "Recommendations on Recognition and Response to Child Abuse and Neglect in the Indian Setting." *Indian Pediatrics*, 47, no. 6 (2010): 493–504. https://doi.org/10.1007/s13312-010-0088-0

11 CRL.A.1415/2012 decided on May 28, 2015.

12 Criminal Appeal No. 1315 of 2015 decided on October 10, 2015.

13 K.C. Faller, "Is the Child Victim of Sexual Abuse Telling the Truth?" *Child Abuse and Neglect*, 8, no. 4 (1984): 473–481. https://doi.org/10.1016/0145-2134(84)90029-2

14 D.G. Beeman, "Child Abuse History and Its Effects on Affect and Social Cognition as Mediated by Social Support." Iowa State University Capstones, available at https://lib.dr.iastate.edu/rtd/9975

15 S.A. Bhat, "Child Sexual Abuse: An Overview." *International Journal of Academic Research and Development*, 2, no. 6 (2017): 271–273. https://doi.org/10.1375/bech.17.1.2

16 *State of Delhi Administration vs. Pannalal* (1993) CriLJ 852 (Delhi).

17 Ibid at 15.

18 Lina Acca Mathew, "Legislative Models of Prosecuting Child Sexual Abuse in India: A Review and Critical Analysis," 2017. Thesis submitted in fulfillment of the requirements for the degree of Doctor of Philosophy at School of Law, Faculty of Law, Queensland University of Technology. https://eprints.qut.edu.au/107784/

19 Ibid.

20 R. Campbell and S. Raja, "Secondary Victimization of Rape Victims: Insights from Mental Health Professionals Who Treat Survivors of Violence." *Violence and Victims*, 14, no. 3 (1999): 261–275. https://doi.org/10.1891/0886-6708.14.3.261

21 L. Ellison, V.E. Munro, K. Hohl and P. Wallang, "Challenging Criminal Justice? Psychosocial Disability and Rape Victimisation." *Criminology & Criminal Justice*, 15, no. 2 (2015): 225–244.

22 M.P. Koss and B.R. Burkhart, "A Conceptual Analysis of Rape Vlctlmlzatlon – Long-Term Effects and Implications for Treatment." *Psychology of Women Quarterly*, 13 (1989): 27–40.

23 I. Kansal, "Child Sexual Abuse in India: Socio-Legal Issues." *International Journal of Scientific Research in Science and Technology*, 2, no. 2 (2016): 126–129, available at https://www.academia.edu/25504138/Child_Sexual_Abuse_in_India_Socio-Legal_Issues

24 N.D. Tapia, "Survivors of Child Sexual Abuse and Predictors of Adult Re-victimization in the United States: A Forward Logistic Regression Analysis." *International Journal of Criminal Justice Sciences*, 9, no. 1 (2014): 64–73, available at https://www.sascv.org/ijcjs/pdfs/Tapiaijcjs2014vol9issue1.pdf

25 Ibid.

26 Ibid at 23.

27 S.W. Faupel, "Etiology of Adult Sexual Offending," available at http://smart.gov/SOMAPI/index

28 R.C. Cronkite and R.H. Moos, "Life Context, Coping Processes, and Depression." In E.E. Beckham and W.R. Leber (eds.), *Handbook of Depression*. 2 (New York: Guilford Press, 1995), 569–587.

29 Canadian Resource Centre for Victims of Crime, "Victim Blaming in Canada," 2022, available at chrome-extension://efaidnbmnnnibpcajpcglclefindmkaj/https://crcvc.ca/wp-content/uploads/2021/09/Victim-Blaming_DISCLAIMER_Revised-April-2022_FINAL.pdf

30 G.L.M. Brotto, G. Sinnamon and W. Petherick, "Victimology and Predicting Victims of Personal Violence," in *The Psychology of Criminal and Antisocial*

Behavior: Victim and Offender Perspectives (Elsevier Inc), 79–144. https://doi.org /10.1016/B978-0-12-809287-3.00003-1

31 Swati Bhatacharjee, ed., *A Unique Crime: Understanding Rape in India* (Gangchil Pub, 2008), 312.

32 Paromita Chattoraj and Sanjukta Sen, *Dilemmas of Responses to Victims of Rape-Psycho-Social and Legal Implications in the Indian Scenario* (Socio legal andro-centrism and gender inequalities) (Eastern Book Company, 2021), 268–288.

33 V. Deswal, "Need to Revisit the Concept of 'Age of Consent'." *Legally Speaking, The Times of India Blogs*, 2019.

34 K. Kanchi, "Criminal Law (Amendment) Act, 2013: Sexual Offences." *Academike*, 2015, available at https://www.lawctopus.com/academike/?s=Criminal+Law+ %28Amendment%29+Act%2C+2013%3A+Sexual+Offences.

35 A. Misra and S. Bronitt, "Reforming Sexual Offences in India: Lessons in Human Rights and Comparative Law." *Griffith Asia Q*, 2 (2014): 37–56.

36 Available at https://indiankanoon.org/doc/87705010/ (Decided on October 11, 10, 2017).

37 S. Jaiswal, "The Prohibition of Child Marriage (Amendment) Bill, 2016," 2016. http://164.100.47.4/billstexts/lsbilltexts/asintroduced/5332LS.pdf

38 V. Anchan, N. Janardhana and J.V.S. Kommu, "POCSO Act, 2012: Consensual Sex as a Matter of Tug of War Between Developmental Need and Legal Obligation for the Adolescents in India." *Indian Journal of Psychological Medicine*, 43, no. 2 (2021, March): 158–162.

39 G. Mantri, *POCSO Criminalizing Teen Sexuality? NCRB Data Suggests that May be True* (Bengaluru: The News Minute, 2019).

40 Centre for Child and Law and National Law School of India University, *Implementation of the POCSO Act, 2012 by Special Courts: Challenges and Issues* (Bengaluru: Centre for Child and Law (CCL) and National Law School of India University (NLSIU), 2018).

41 H.C. Whittle, C. Hamilton-Giachritsis and A.R. Beech, "Victims' Voices: The Impact of Online Grooming and Sexual Abuse." *Universal Journal of Psychology*, 1 (2013): 59–71.

42 (1995) 1 SCC 14 at 17.

43 A. Romen Kumar Singh, "Ignoring the Rights of Rape Victim," available at http:// www.ifp.co.in/nws-11963-ignoring-the-rights-of-rape-victim/ (visited on April 3, 2012).

44 S. 154. CrPC- Information in cognizable cases.

45 Office of Victims of Crime, "Basic Guidelines on Approaching Victims of Crime," 2020, available at https://www.ncjrs.gov/ovc_archives/reports/firstrep/bgavoc .html.

46 N. Jain and A. Tyagi, "State of Rape Victims in India," *Elementary Education Online*, 19, no. 4 (2020): 6241–6247. https://doi.org/10.17051/ilkonline.2020.04 .765030

47 M. Laxminarayan, "Procedural Justice and Psychological Effects of Criminal Proceedings: The Moderating Effect of Offense Type." *Social Justice Research*, 25 (2012): 390–405. https://doi.org/10.1007/s11211-012-0167-6

48 M.R. Sable et al., "Barriers to Reporting Sexual Assault for Women and Men." *Journal of American College Health*, 55, no. 3 (2006): 157–162, available at http:// www.middlebury.edu/media/view/240971/authentic/sable_article.pdf

49 National Commission on Protection of Child Rights, available at https://ncpcr.gov .in/ (visited on July 31, 2023).

50 *One Stop Centre Scheme*. (n.d.). Vikaspedia, available at https://vikaspedia.in/ social-welfare/women-and-child-development/women-development-1/one-stop -centre-scheme (Retrieved June 13, 2023).

51 Ministry of Women & Child Develpoment, "Ministry of Women & Child Development One Stop Centres Scheme," 2016, available at http://mahilaehaat-rmk.gov.in/
52 S. 164A CrPC- Medical Examination of a victim of rape.
53 1981 AIR 1122, 1981 SCR (3) 259.
54 CASE NO.: Appeal (CRL.) 522 of 1999.
55 M.A. No. 1852 of 2019 in Crl. App. No. 1101.
56 (*"Everyone Blames Me"* *Barriers to Justice and Support Services for Sexual Assault Survivors in India,* n.d.).
57 Josse, E. (2010). They Came with Two Guns: The Consequences of Sexual Violence for the Mental Health of Women in Armed Conflicts. *International Review of the Red Cross, 92*(877), 177–195. https://doi.org/doi:10.1017/S1816383110000251.
58 Ibid.
59 Section 228A IPC- Disclosure of the identity of the victim in certain cases.
60 (2003) 8 SCC 551.
61 Criminal Appeal No. 1581 of 2009.
62 Writ Petition (Civil) No. 565 of 2012.
63 (1996) 2 SCC 384.
64 Crime in India statistics, National Crime Records Bureau (NCRB).
65 Section 23 of the POCSO Act – Procedure for media.
66 Sec. 33 of the POCSO Act – Procedure and powers of the Special Court.
67 S. Chaudhury et al., "Psychological Aspects of Rape and Its Consequences." *Psychology and Behavioral Science International Journal, 2,* no. 3 (2017). https://doi.org/10.19080/pbsij.2017.02.555586
68 P. Chattoraj, "Chapter 4: PREVALENCE OF RAPE and EVOLUTION OF RAPE LAWS IN INDIA – Bridging the Gap between 'Is' and 'Ought'." Kalinga Institute of Industrial Technology, available at https://library.kiit.ac.in/digital-library/
69 T. Callender and L. Dartnall, "Mental Health Responses for Victims of Sexual Violence and Rape in Resource-Poor Settings." *Sexual Violence Research Initiative,* (2002): 1–12, available at https://www.ciaonet.org/attachments/19594/uploads
70 I. Areh, G. Mešico and P. Umek, "Attribution of Personal Characteristics to Victims of Rape - Police Officers' Perspectives." *Studia Psychologica,* 51, no. 1 (2009): 85–100.
71 Sec. 357 CrPC – Order to pay compensation.
72 G. Sandhya. (2019). *Compensation to Rape Victims- A Critical Analysis.* The Criminal Law Blog b by National Law University, Jodhpur. https://criminallawstud iesnluj.wordpress.com/2019/08/30/compensation-to-rape-victims-a-critical-analysis/ Last visited on 22-11-2023.
73 Sec. 357A CrPC – Victim Compensation Scheme.
74 Compensation Scheme for Women Victims/Survivors of Sexual Assault/other Crime 2018.
75 Writ Petition (Civil) No. 565/2012) (2019) 13 SCC 715.
76 Writ Petition (Crl.) 3244/2019, dated June 15, 2020.
77 W.P. (CRL) 1419/2020 (Date of decision May 13, 2021).
78 Child Welfare Information Gateway, available at https://www.childwelfare.gov (visited on July 31, 2023).
79 NSPCC, available at https://www.nspcc.org.uk/ (visited on July 31, 2023).
80 K. Ehliasson and U. Markström, "Revealing the Ideas in the Swedish Social Services Act Regarding Support to Individuals with Disabilities." *Scandinavian Journal of Disability Research,* 22, no. 1 (2020): 393–402. https://doi.org/10.16993/SJDR.720
81 United Nations Office on Drugs and Crime, "Handbook on Effective Prosecution Responses to Violence against Women and Girls," available at chrome-extension://efaidnbmnnnibpcajpcglclefindmkaj/https://www.unodc.org/documents/justice-and

-prison-reform/V1402565-HB_on_effective_prosecution_responses_to_violence
_against_women_and_girls.pdf
82   Cassia Spohn, "Specialized Units and Vertical Prosecution Approaches," in Ronald
F. Wright, Kay L. Levine and Russell M. Gold (eds.), *The Oxford Handbook of
Prosecutors and Prosecution* (2021; online edn, Oxford Academic, April 14, 2021).
https://doi.org/10.1093/oxfordhb/9780190905422.013.13 (accessed July 31, 2023).
83   S. Agnihotri and M. Das, "Reviewing India's Protection of Children from Sexual
Offences Act Three Years On," (2015): 2–5, available at http://eprints.lse.ac.uk
/74845/1/blogs.lse.ac.uk-Reviewing India's Protection of Children from Sexual
Offences Act three years on.pdf
84   Mathew, "Legislative Models of Prosecuting Child Sexual Abuse in India."
85   Bhadra Sinha, "Victim can Engage Lawyer in Criminal Trial, but not for Arguments:
SC." *Hindustan Times*, November 21, 2019, available at https://www.hindustanti-
mes.com/india-news/victim-can-engage-lawyer-in-criminal-trial-but-not-for-argu-
ments-sc/story-ViQZs0GepxeZTe9tGRpR5O.html
86   B.F. Vik, K. Rasmussen, B. Schei and C.T. Hagemann, "Is Police Investigation
of Rape Biased by Characteristics of Victims?" *Forensic Science International:
Synergy*, 2 (2020): 98–106. https://doi.org/10.1016/j.fsisyn.2020.02.003
87   Amy Klobuchar, "Eye on Interrogations: How Videotaping Serves the Cause of
Justice." *Washington Post*, June 10, 2002.
88   Ibid.
89   Section 43 POCSO Act - Public awareness about Act
90   Section 44 of Pocso Act 2012 - Monitoring of implementation of Act

3 Role of police in investigation of sexual offences against children

Introduction

Any community that wants to advance needs peace and favourable conditions. Anarchic and disturbed cultures invest all of their potential in worthless endeavours. On the other side, citizens can grow and succeed if they feel comfortable, secure, and in control. Because of this, the police play a crucial role in maintaining the security and safety of society. This structure has always existed in some shape or another, with different roles and responsibilities.[1]

The law in India is upheld by several organizations. In contrast to many federal countries, the constitution of India gives the states and territories primary responsibility for upholding the law. Some of India's paramilitary forces are employed by the Ministry of Home Affairs at the federal level to aid the states.[2] The state police in each state have police forces in larger cities. Without efficient implementation, the creation of laws is only an abstract concept; thus all of the criminal justice system's organs must work together to ensure that the system is fully functional.[3]

Perpetration of sexual offences is symbolic as failure of not only the law and order but also the basic feeling of security among the citizens. Most of the sexual offences under the Indian legal regime are dealt under the Indian Penal Code 1860 (IPC), and child sexual offences cases are specifically dealt under the POCSO Act. Both of these laws are central laws, i.e., applicable throughout the territory of India. The police in India perform multifarious activities, from responding to emergency situations to the most routine activities of patrolling duties. The role, responsibilities, and powers of the police have been redefined in the second report of the National Police Commission (1977–81).[4] To begin with, the police must conduct investigations into crimes, apprehend offenders, and take part in any related legal proceedings in order to respond to crimes. They must also identify issues and circumstances that are likely to lead to the commission of crimes. The police's preventive role entails minimizing the likelihood that crimes will be committed through proactive patrolling and other sensible police measures, assisting and collaborating with other relevant agencies for the prevention of crimes, and creating and maintaining a sense of security in the community. In addition to these services,

DOI: 10.4324/9781003345244-3

police also help those who are in physical danger, ease traffic flow for people and cars, offer other necessary services in an emergency, and provide comfort to those who are in distress. More crucially, police work to gather information on issues that impact public order and crimes in general, such as social and economic offences.[5]

In light of the broad roles of the police as discussed above the goal of the police as the first responders to sexual offences against adults and especially against children becomes indispensable.[6] Sexual abuse against children leaves many long-lasting effects on victims including pain, fear, self-harm, feelings of guilt and shame, post-traumatic stress disorder (PTSD), impaired brain development, suicidal attempts, difficulties during adolescence, abusive behaviour, and sexually transmitted diseases.[7] The physical effects add to the emotional and mental damage as an outcome of the abuse. Sexual abuse against a child destroys the mindset of the child and thrusts the child into an emotional crisis. The immediate and predominant impact of such sexual abuse is of shock. There are wide-ranging effects of sexual abuse, and there is no single symptom that is present in all victims.[8] Children who have experienced sexual abuse are severely let down by the criminal justice system's systematic inability to address their concerns as well as by the stigma attached to such abuse in society.

Although it is still frowned upon, child sexual abuse is a very serious issue in India, where the lack of strong regulations and the stigma attached to the crime have made matters worse. Most people believe that this is primarily a problem of the West that does not exist in India. The term *child sexual abuse* has different meanings in different countries. In practically all industrialized countries, crimes against children are punishable by law. In India, despite the Directive Principles of State Policy in the Indian Constitution speaking of protecting the rights of children under Articles 39(e) and Article 39(f), it has the highest number of child sex workers in the world.[9] In India, sexual abuse of children has become an unseen crime due to disbelief, denial, and cover-ups for the sake of family reputation and it is as ancient as the patriarchy and joint family structure.

Before the passing of the POCSO Act, sexual offence against a girl child was only recognized by the law under the general substantive provision of the Section 375 IPC, i.e., the rape provision. According to the Crime in India statistics 2021, the ratio of boy child victims to the girl child victim is approximately 1:93, i.e., for every incident of child sexual abuse being reported involving a boy child victim, there are 93 incidents of girl child victims that are being reported. Ever since the passing of the POCSO Act, 90% of the sexual offence cases against children involves a girl child and therefore automatically it is read as a rape case under the IPC as well. However, the rape myths have been recognized as one of the important reasons behind the attrition at the investigative stage.[10] Historically, which is why the rape victims have been mistreated by criminal justice systems.[11] In the same way, the decision of the judge to trust the victim is determined by their own perception from the attributes of the victim both during rape and the trial.[12]

The grievances of the victims of sexual abuse take numerous forms as they approach the criminal justice system.[13] Harassment, delay, adjournments, repeated court appearances, aggressive questioning, etc. cause secondary victimization of the child victim.[14] In India the breach of sexual autonomy is often linked to the reputation of the family thereby in sexual assault cases, the trend of underreporting is quite common.[15] The importance of implementing the pro-victim provisions in the POCSO Act cannot be undermined since the authorities, to lay their hands on the perpetrator, have to first set the procedures right for the victim.[16] Throughout the process of criminal justice administration, victims experience the need for legal guidance and support, in the absence of which, they go through the procedures without readiness and uncertainty.[17]

Medical examination is an indispensable part of the investigation of sexual offence cases. And in case of a child victim, the duty of the doctor while conducting the medical examination of the child is to interpret trauma, collect specimen, treat injury, and, above all, help and support the vulnerable patient.[18] It has also been observed in the United States that by employing the model of Sexual Assault Nurse Examiner programmes the rate of guilty pleas or convictions could have been statistically improved.[19]

One-Stop Centers (OSCs) scheme otherwise known as the Sakhi Centers are implemented in India since April 1st, 2015. According to the scheme, they are obliged to be situated within a 2-kilometre radius of the hospital grounds and must provide women who have experienced abuse with a variety of integrated services under one roof, including police facilitation, medical assistance, legal assistance, and counselling.

When it comes to the functioning of OSCs in the states of Odisha, Jharkhand and West Bengal, Odisha and Jharkhand have functional OSCs for every district as opposed to WB where the functioning of OSCs is non-existent.[20] Pacifying the ordeal of sexual offences for the victim is as vital as trying the guilty.[21] But for the system to work at par to punish the guilty, sensitization of various organs involved is of utmost importance.[22]

Investigation of rape and sexual offences against children cases

The process of investigation in cases of sexual offences of children begins with the reporting of the offence and proceeds towards the submission of the investigation report to the Special Court (in POCSO cases) by the police.

Figure 3.1 depicts the stages of investigation generally involved in cases of rape and child sexual abuse.

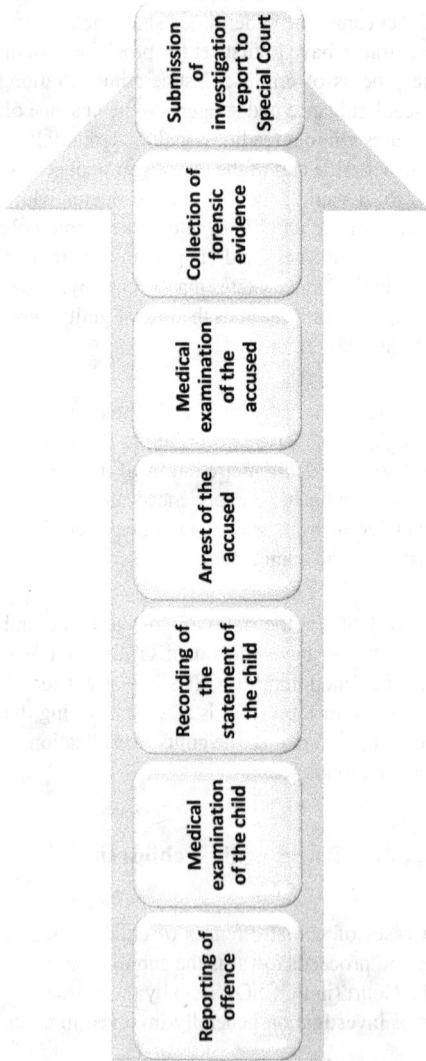

Figure 3.1 Investigation process in cases of rape and sexual offences against children.

Chapter XII of the CrPC talks of giving information to the police and their powers to investigate a case. This chapter deals with their powers related to investigation of offences that includes, examination of witness, medical examination, search, inquiry and report on suicide, etc. These powers are intrinsic and not given to them to intrude or encroach into the privacy by any means. Sections 154–176 of CrPC explain about the procedures of investigation.

Therefore, the process of investigation in rape and sexual offences against children broadly involves registering the information; recording the statement of the victims and other relevant witnesses; medical examination of the victims and the accused person(s); search and seizure of material evidence, including forensic evidence like (semen, hair, nail, blood, etc.); sending the forensic samples to the forensic laboratories for analysis and collecting the report of the same; arrest of the accused person; and recording of statements by the Magistrate (admissions of witnesses including the victim and confession of accused (if any).

The steps of investigation by the police in cases of sexual offences against children can be stated as follows:

Reporting of an offence

Under Section 154 Criminal Procedure Code (CrPC), any information given to the police Officer-in-Charge (OIC) of the police station in case of a cognizable offence[23] shall have to be registered by him which is the First Information Report (FIR). The information can be given orally or in writing, and shall be signed by the person authorizing it. In cases of offences against women (acid attacks, sexual harassment, rape (of all kinds) such evidence should be mandatorily noted by a woman officer of the police station. Failure to register such offences by the police may also invite penal liability u/s 166A IPC.

The Bharatiya Nagarik Suraksha Sanhita, 2023 (BNSS), New Criminal Procedure Bill) (Bill No. 122 of 2023) recognizes reporting of offences to the OIC of the police station using digital medium, but it has to be signed by the person reporting within three days of giving the information.

Reporting of an offence committed under the POCSO Act is governed by S. 19 of the POCSO Act. It puts the responsibility on any person including a child to inform the commission of an offence under the Act to the Special Juvenile Police Units (SJPUs) or the local police station. When a child provides information, it must be written down simply and, if necessary, the child against whom the offence has been committed must be taken to the nearest shelter, home, or hospital, as appropriate, within twenty-four hours of providing the information. The SJPU or the local police as the case may be, have also been ordered to inform the Special Court or the Court of Sessions of the actions taken in this respect.

The NCRB data on Crimes against children reveal that 98.89% of POCSO victims are females (average data from 2017–2021) and in such cases the

Table 3.1 Number of cases reported in the selected states under the POCSO Act

Year	Odisha	Jharkhand	West Bengal
2020	2202	938	2657
2019	2036	654	2267
2018	1887	615	2267
2017	249	385	2131
2016	1928	348	2132
2015	19	141	1289
2014	109	31	1058

Note: Author's own compilation.

mandates given under S. 154 CrPC regarding reporting of information have to be complied with by the police as the first responder.

In offences against women which generally includes acid attack, disrobing, voyeurism, outraging a woman's modesty, and specifically sexual offences like sexual harassment and all the recognized forms of rape under the IPC and the POCSO Act, any woman officer of the police station is mandated to record such information and the statement of the victim.

The strict mandate of the law for permitting only woman officers to be the first persons to face and respond to the victims of rape is due to the apparent apathy of male police personnel and shaming of the victims by them, which makes the victim reluctant to reach out to the criminal justice machinery even on the face of immense suffering. The law also provides that in case the victim is temporarily or permanently physically or mentally incapacitated then such recording should be done at a place of convenience of the victim in presence of special instructors or interpreters with videography. The official statistics (Table 3.1) shows an alarming picture regarding a steady rise in the CSA cases since 2014 in the three states where the authors collected data on rape and POCSO cases from the sample police stations ($n=211$).

Case study

The empirical study by the authors revealed that in spite of the law mandating any woman officer of the police station to record the FIR u/s 154 CrPC and the statement of the victim (as a witness under s. 161 CrPC), it was admitted by the IOs that in almost 25% of the police in OD, 16% in JH, and 31% in WB they functioned without any woman officer. Notably, 82% of the police stations in

OD, 94% in JH, and 44% in WB admitted to not having the information registered by any woman officer. In total, 97% of the police stations in OD stated that the lack of women officers is the main reason for the non-registration of rape cases by a woman officer. It was thought-provoking to note that in spite of a clear provision in the law, the IOs in many police stations admitted their ignorance by stating that rape cases like other criminal cases case can be registered by the IIC or the OIC of a police station even though they are not woman officers.

But from the data of National Crime Records Bureau 2019,[24] the figures from the three states showed that West Bengal police had the lowest caseload in a year per woman officer (1:0.4), followed by Jharkhand (1:0.5) and Odisha (1:0.6). Although the departmental allocation of the number of woman officers per police stations is not known, it was clear from the data that the number of woman officers in Odisha was 9 for each police station, whereas in Jharkhand it was 11 and in West Bengal it was 14, that is, at least one lady officer per police station could be easily made available. This contradicts the response given by officers, where in about 25% cases in Odisha, 16% in Jharkhand, and 31% in West Bengal have said that there are not even a single woman officer in such stations.

Mandatory reporting of sexual offences against children

Since the enactment of the POCSO Act, everyone now bears the responsibility to report sexual offences against minors. The POCSO Act defines a number of offences, including sexual harassment, aggravated and non-aggravated penetrative assault, sexual assault, and the exploitation of a minor for pornographic usages. Employees of hospitals, the media, lodges, hotels, or photography facilities also have an express responsibility to report u/s 20 of the POCSO Act, and they have to notify the police or the SJPU if they come across any sexually explicit materials. A doctor who suspects a child who has been abused sexually is required by Rule 3.2 of the Model Guidelines of the POCSO Act, 2012, to report the commission of an offence under the said Act to the police directly or to their superiors, who will then inform it to the police later. Under the POCSO Act, failing to report the conduct of a sexual offence is punished by up to six months in jail, a fine, or both. However, children are not subject to punishment for failing to report a crime. The Act also mandates that the person in charge of a business or organization to notify any potential offences committed by subordinates. Failing to do so carries a possible one-year jail sentence and a fine. The POCSO Act 2012 clearly says that no one would face the responsibility of any sort for providing information in good belief concerning the actual commission, or the risk of commission, of a sexual crime as a protection for individuals reporting an incident. Section 52 of the IPC defines the phrase good faith as: "*Nothing is said to be done or believed in good faith which is done or believed without due care and attention.*" Thus, before reporting a case of sexual offence against a minor to the police, the reporter is required to have taken reasonable care and attention. However, the Act does not absolve an individual of the responsibility if the incident is reported to a supervisor or another authority other than the police. The responsibility to report is seen as a way to acknowledge the gravity and prevalence of child sexual abuse as well as a way to stop further harm. Imposing the need to report the offences guarantees that these incidents are revealed, allowing the victim to be taken out of the abusive situation and have the chance to seek professional and/or medical aid, as well as the perpetrator to be charged with a crime and stop further sexual assault. This is crucial since most cases of sexual abuse and violence go unreported and because children are typically powerless to defend themselves or bring the offender to justice. The idea of mandatory reporting consequently reinforces the moral imperative that exists to safeguard children from harm. The POCSO Act also mandates that incidents of sexual offences against minors be reported to the authorities, holding the community at large responsible for doing so. Despite the fact that the phrase mandatory reporting does not appear in the POCSO Act, it is clear from Section 21 that the reporting requirement is mandatory. This section outlines the penalties for failing to report a sexual offence, with the exception that no child can be held accountable.

In the case of *State of Maharashtra vs Dr. Maroti s/o Kashinath Pimpalkar*[25] the Supreme Court observed that "*non-reporting of sexual assault against a minor child despite knowledge is a serious crime. More often than not, it is an attempt to shield the offenders of the crime of sexual assault.*" However, creating an exception, the SC in a case relating to a minor seeking for a termination of pregnancy under the Medical Termination of Pregnancy Act 1971 in X vs Principal Secretary, Health and Family Welfare Department, Govt of NCT Of Delhi[26] noted that minors may be less likely to seek out Registered Medical Practitioners (RMPs) for safe termination of their pregnancies under Rule 3(b) of the Medical Termination of Pregnancy Rule 2003 if there is a need of disclosing of the minor's name in the report under Section 19(1) of POCSO; as a result, the RMP may only disclose the minor's identity and other personal information upon request from the minor and the minor's guardian.

However, it was interesting to find from the data collected in the three states that not a single case had been registered by the police stations, for failure to report sexual offence cases under the mandatory reporting provisions in all the 211 police stations since POCSO Act was enforced.

Exception to police's powers to require attendance of witness

The police can generally call the witnesses of a crime (including victim), at the police station for giving their statements (section 160 CrPC). The proviso introduced in 2013 exempts *any male below fifteen years* or *any woman* (these categories of witnesses will cover victims of rape and CSA) or a *psychologically and physically disabled person* from coming to the police station.

This exclusion shows that the lawmakers recognize that the police stations in India can be intimidating for the vulnerable victim and such exclusion by the law lets him/her to give their statement as a witness at a place where she may be more comfortable.

Recording of statement of the victim by the police

The IO may question the witnesses of the case in accordance with Section 161 of the CrPC. The police may write down the statement obtained during the examination, establish a separate true record of each witness' testimony, and record the stated statement using audio or video technology. Under section 24, the POCSO Act provides the procedure for recording of the evidence of the child by the IO. According to the law, a woman officer with a minimum rank of Sub-Inspector shall take the child's statement and record it in the victim's home or another convenient location. This clause imposes certain duties on the police, including the requirement that the officer not be in uniform, that the child never interact with the abuser while being questioned, that no child be kept in the police station after dark for any reason, and, lastly, that the child remain anonymous to the media unless the Court orders otherwise. Guidelines for interviewing children are discussed in Chapter 3 of the Model Guidelines under Section 39 of the POCSO Act, 2012.

It emphasizes the requirement for assessors to be made more sensitive in order to prevent the interview procedure from upsetting the child.

Case study

Chapter 6 of the POCSO Act states the process of registering the account of the child victim by the police at the residence or any new place of convenience of the victim. However, it was also stated by the majority of the police stations that the convenience of the victim is given the utmost importance. However, from the responses of the police interviewed in Odisha (97%) Jharkhand (32%) and West Bengal (85%), the police admitted to having recorded such statements at the police station. The obligation on the police officer regarding the presence of the guardian and the restriction of wearing uniform during recording the statement of the child were being mostly said to be complied with.

The data collection revealed that there were numerous police stations in the three states which functioned without any woman police officers. The IOs further admitted that in such circumstances, a requisition is sent to the nearest police station for a woman officer. And such a woman officer records the statement of the child victim and proceeds ahead with the investigation.

Medical examination

Of the victim

The medical examination of the victim is a significant step in the collection of valuable evidence when it concerns sexual offences.

It has been provided in section 164A CrPC that a RMP (registered medical practitioner) working in a hospital managed by the government or the local authority and in the absence of such practitioner any other doctor has to examine the rape victim or with whom an attempt of rape has been committed. It is only with the permission of the victim or any person who is authorized to give permission on her behalf that the examination can be conducted.

In order to guarantee that the minor is given proper care and to assist in the legal decision-making process, the medical examination of a case of suspected child sexual abuse is a crucial component of a thorough response to the inquiry.[27] An appropriate medical evaluation can be comforting for the child and the professionals involved as well as address immediate medical concerns.[28] The appropriate determination, certification, and clarification of the conclusions on the basis of the medical examination conducted can have major implications for the protection of the victims.[29] And at the same time proper sensitization of the medical professionals dealing with cases of sexual abuse against children should not be done away with.[30]

Section 27 of the POCSO Act mandates that a female medical professional evaluate a girl child victim in front of the parent or any other adult in whom the child has shown confidence. Additionally, the medical examination must be done with a woman in attendance who has been chosen by the hospital chief if the child's parent is unable to attend the examination. Under the aforementioned Act and the POCSO Rules 2020, it is not necessary to file a FIR in order to examine the minor victim medically.

The provision of medical care and aid to the victim is dealt under Rule 6 of the POCSO Rules 2020. On receiving the information of an offence committed under said Act, the officer of the SJPU or the local police shall take the child victim to the nearest medical facility for immediate medical attention. The emergency medical care shall be rendered to the victim in the presence of the guardian and the anonymity of the victim shall be maintained at all times. The RMP attending the victim shall attend to the needs of cuts and bruises, contact with sexually transmitted diseases, exposure to HIV, possible pregnancy etc. and provide appropriate treatment suiting as per the needs of the child victim. The RMP is under the obligation submit a report to the SJPU or the local police on the condition of the child victim within twenty-four hours of such treatment.

Similarly, the guidelines for medical and healthcare professionals while dealing with a case under POCSO is dealt under Chapter 3 of Model Guidelines under Section 39 of the POCSO Act.

Of the accused

The medical examination of the accused must be completed as soon as possible since it is just as crucial as the examination of the victim. A person accused of committing a rape is required under S. 53A CrPC to submit to a medical examination by a RMP working for a government hospital or local authority, or by any other medical professional located within 16 kilometres of the alleged crime's scene. Furthermore, if the accused refuses to participate with the medical examination, reasonable force may be employed.

Case study

With respect to the data received from the police interviewed, it was understood that for the victims the medical examination was conducted within 24 hours of them reporting the offence and for the accused, they were taken for the medical examination within 24 hours of making the arrest. The responses of the police showed a 100% compliance of the mandate of conducting the medical examination of a girl child victim by a lady doctor in Jharkhand, Odisha (92%), and West Bengal (62%). The non-compliance is primarily due to a lack of registered women doctors in the nearest medical facilities, which could not be verified from independent sources. The law being silent on the consequences of non-compliance of this provision leads to a situation where the police and the hospitals shift the burden on one another. Odisha showed the highest adherence at 100% followed by West Bengal at 97% and lastly by Jharkhand at 86% to the mandate of conducting the said examination of the child in the presence of the guardian.

The medical examination of the accused is usually conducted within 24 hours of the arrest as revealed from the responses of the police officers who were interviewed (100% in Odisha, 96% in Jharkhand, and 89% in West Bengal).

Forensic evidence

The gathering of forensic evidence during a sexual crime investigation plays a significant role in the investigative process and offers workable answers to the current criminal conditions.[31] Forensic evidence plays a pivotal part in establishing the truth in rape and other sexual offence cases provided there is proper collection, storage, and maintenance of a chain of custody that will prove the authenticity of such evidence. In addition, the Verma Committee Report in 2013 recommended the usage of Sexual Assault Forensic Examination (SAFE) kits for collecting the evidence from the body of the victim and the accused. Such a standardized protocol of collection and storage of evidence will not allow the defence to question the credibility of the forensic evidence during trial.

Although human interaction at various phases of the management of forensic materials and testing has considerable opportunity for contamination, manipulation, and frauds, science does not utter falsehoods.[32] First responders to the scene of crime and the bodies of the victims and the accused must be trained in order to avoid loss or contamination of evidence. The main component in ensuring the forensic sample's validity is the chain of custody.[33] According to the protocol, it is possible to avoid modification and contamination of biological samples while they are being collected, packaged, stored, and transported from the crime scene to the lab. Lack of uniform guidelines chain of custody for handling forensic samples provides plenty of opportunities for diluting the case of the prosecution and therefore weakening it. The collection of forensic evidence from the RMP shall be as per S. 27 of the POCSO Act according to Rule 6(6) of the POCSO Rules 2020.

Case study

It was only in Jharkhand that 84% of the police stated that SAFE kits were being used for the collection of evidence from the victim and the accused, while 98% of the police in Odisha and 55% of the police in West Bengal stated otherwise. The procedure of collection of evidence from the bodies of the victim and the accused is being done by the Registered Medical Practitioners. The modus operandi of sending of samples for forensic analysis was found to be different in different jurisdictions. In Odisha, the samples were collected by the police from the hospitals and immediately sealed in the presence of a Magistrate and then sent for forensic analysis to the concerned Forensic Science Laboratory (FSL) (District FSL/Regional FSL/State FSL). In the state of West Bengal, Kolkata Police were forwarding the samples and under West Bengal police jurisdiction the samples were being forwarded by the Magistrate. The CrPC or the POCSO have not bestowed any obligation on the Magistrate in terms of forwarding of forensic evidence; so it was not clear how the Magistrates may be involved in forwarding of samples for forensic analysis. While in Jharkhand no clear picture of the modus operandi of sending the samples could be obtained.

One of the primary reasons for not considering forensic evidence as a standalone substantive piece of evidence by the judges is due to the fact that there is no standard protocol for collection, storage, and transmission of the samples collected from the victims and the accused upon medical examination without any loss of time to the forensic laboratories. There have been instances where samples have been stored in the police stations without refrigeration facilities and without maintaining any chain of custody by the personnel handling the sample. All of these factors lead to spoilage of samples or manipulation in handling of samples that gives an opportunity to the defence to question the credibility of a forensic report during the trial. The judicial attitude in using forensic evidence in the trial of sexual offences is discussed in detail in the subsequent chapter. This is the major reason why judges are apprehensive of considering forensic evidence without corroboration by any other evidences.

Arrest of the accused

An arrest implies the act of taking a person into custody when they may be suspected of a crime or offence.

It is usually done in case of a cognizable offence when reasonable suspicion on the basis of credible information is received (section 41 CrPC) Further, section 57 CrPC safeguards the rights of the arrestee by providing that the police officer must produce the arrestee before the magistrate having jurisdiction of the case within twenty-four hours of making such arrest.

The POCSO Act is a unique legislation with provisions that supersede those of the CrPC. The methods outlined in the special legislation shall take precedence over the general legislation, and in the absence of any such provision, the process outlined in the CrPC may be applicable, according to a saving clause included in section 5 of the CrPC. In effect, the CrPC would only be applicable if there is no similar provision in the special legislation. As the POCSO Act does not provide for arrest provisions, which means the CrPC provisions shall apply. Generally, arrests can be made with a warrant (in non-cognizable cases) and without it (in cognizable cases) under the CrPC. According to Section 19 of the POCSO Act, there is a unique mechanism for reporting violations; however, it is not specified in the Act whether the offences are cognizable or not. The CrPC must be consulted to decide whether an offence is cognizable or not in the absence of any such specific provision.

According to the First Schedule of the CrPC, if an offence is punishable by imprisonment for three years or less, a fine, or both, it will be considered as non-cognizable offences. However, if it is punishable by imprisonment for three years or more including life imprisonment or death penalty, or both, it will be considered as a cognizable offence.

The POCSO Act's list of offences mentioned below can help us determine if the offences under the said Act are cognizable or non-cognizable (Table 3.2).

Case study

The interviews of the police officers revealed that the attitudes of the police differed slightly when it came to arresting the accused. While the police in Odisha stated that they usually arrest the accused on receiving the information from the victim (after the registration of the FIR), the police in Jharkhand and WB stated that on having a reasonable suspicion, they arrest the accused. While used differently by the police of different jurisdictions, the terms registration of FIR and "on reasonable suspicion" both connote towards the receipt of some information by the police regarding the commission of the crime.

Table 3.2 Classification of offences under the POCSO Act

Section	Offence	Punishment	Cognizable/ Non-cognizable	Bailable/Non-bailable	Triable by what court
4	Penetrative sexual assault	Imprisonment for 7 years upto life	Cognizable"	Non-bailable	Court of Sessions
6	Aggravated penetrative sexual assault	Rigorous imprisonment for 10 years upto life and fine	Cognizable	Non-bailable	Court of Sessions
8	Sexual assault	Imprisonment for 3 years upto 5 years	Cognizable	Non-bailable	Magistrate of the first class
10	Aggravated sexual assault	Imprisonment for 5 years upto 7 years	Cognizable	Non-bailable	Magistrate of the first class
12	Sexual harassment	Imprisonment upto 3 years and fine	Non-cognizable	Bailable	Any Magistrate
14(1)	Use of child for pornographic purposes	Imprisonment upto 5 years and fine Second conviction- Imprisonment upto 7 years	Cognizable	Non-bailable	Magistrate of the first class
14(2)	Use of child for pornographic purposes and commits the offence of penetrative sexual assault	Imprisonment for not less than 10 years upto life and fine	Cognizable	Non-bailable	Court of Sessions
14(2)	Use of child for pornographic purposes and commits the offence of aggravated penetrative sexual assault	Rigorous imprisonment for life and fine	Cognizable	Non-bailable	Court of Sessions
14(2)	Use of child for pornographic purposes and commits the offence of sexual assault	Imprisonment for 6 years upto 8 years and fine	Cognizable	Non-bailable	Court of Sessions

(Continued)

Table 3.2 (Continued)

Section	Offence	Punishment	Cognizable/ Non-cognizable	Bailable/Non-bailable	Triable by what court
14(2)	Use of child for pornographic purposes and commits the offence of aggravated sexual assault	Imprisonment for 8 years upto 10 years and fine	Cognizable	Non-bailable	Court of Sessions
15(1)	Storage of pornographic material involving a child fails to delete or destroy or report the same to the designated authority	Fine upto Rs. 5000 Subsequent offence – Fine upto Rs. 10,000	Cognizable	Non-bailable	Magistrate of the first class
15(2)	Storage of pornographic material involving a child for the purposes of displaying or distributing in any manner	Imprisonment upto 3 years and fine	Cognizable	Non-bailable	Magistrate of the first class
15(3)	Storage of pornographic material involving a child for commercial purposes	Imprisonment for 3 years upto 5 years with fine Subsequent conviction – Imprisonment for 5 years up to 7 years with fine	Cognizable	Non-bailable	Magistrate of the first class
17	Abetment of an offence u/the Act	Punishment provided for that offence	Depends on the offence abetted	Depends on the offence abetted	Depends on the offence abetted
18	Attempt to commit an offence u/the Act	Punishment for a description provided for the offence up to one-half of the imprisonment for life, one-half of the longest term of imprisonment provided for that offence with fine	Depends on the offence attempted to have been committed	Depends on the offence attempted to have been committed	Depends on the offence attempted to have been committed

(Continued)

Table 3.2 (Continued)

Section	Offence	Punishment	Cognizable/ Non-cognizable	Bailable/Non-bailable	Triable by what court
21	Failure to report or record a case- Any person	Imprisonment upto 6 months with fine	Non-cognizable	Bailable	Any Magistrate
21	Failure to report or record a case-Any person in charge of an institution	Imprisonment upto 12 months with fine	Non-cognizable	Bailable	Any Magistrate
22 (1)	False complaint/ false information regarding offences u/s 3, 5, 7, 9 of the Act	Imprisonment upto 6 months with fine	Non-cognizable	Bailable	Any Magistrate
22(3)	False complaint/false information for victimizing the child	Imprisonment upto 12 months with fine	Non-cognizable	Bailable	Any Magistrate
23	Violations on part of the media	Imprisonment for 6 months upto one year and fine	Non-cognizable	Bailable	Any Magistrate

Submission of investigation report

Finally, according to Section 173 of the CrPC, any investigation conducted in accordance with this chapter must be finished promptly. Additionally, it is mentioned that the investigation into a crime under Sections 376, 376A, 376AB, 376B, 376C, 376D, 376DA, 376DB, and 376E of the IPC must be finished within two months of the day the information was registered by the OIC of the police station.

This step signifies a symbolic completion of the investigation by the police. Under the BNSS Bill, the obligation has been placed on the IO to inform the victim or the informant about the progression of the case within 90 days by any means including electronic medium.

As the POCSO Act lacks a provision regarding the submission of investigation report, section 173 of CrPC shall be relied upon while submitting an investigation report on the completion of the investigation. Similarly, as no duration for completing the investigation is provided under the POCSO Act, it might follow that in case of sexual offences against a girl child, which is also the offence of rape u/s 375 IPC, the period of 2 months or 60 days for completing the investigation (u/s 173 (1A) CrPC) should be complied with. However, in cases of offences against a male child, the above provision of section 173 (1A) CrPC shall not apply and in such cases section 167 CrPC will come into play that provides that the investigation of an offence punishable with less than 10 years shall be completed within 60 days and more than 10 years, including life imprisonment and death, shall be 90 days, failing which the accused if in custody will be released on bail. This creates a dichotomous situation where the duration of the investigation varies in case of a sexual offence against a girl and a boy child.

Case study

Findings from the empirical study revealed that the police in the three states filed charge sheet for the offence of rape within two months. It is only in situations that the accused is absconding, and there is a delay in the submission of the charge sheet.

Summary of procedural laws for investigation of cases of sexual offences against children

The POCSO Act 2012 is the special law for dealing with the cases of sexual offences against children. In the absence of a provision in the POCSO Act, the CrPC is followed. In addition to the POCSO Act, the POCSO Rules 2020

Table 3.3 Summary of procedures for investigation and trial of sexual abuse of a child

	CrPC	POCSO Act 2012	POCSO Rules 2020	Model Guidelines for POCSO 2012
Reporting/ Registration of offence	S. 154	S.19	No specific provision	No specific provision
Recording of the statement of the victim	S. 161	S. 24, 26	No specific provision	Chapter 3
Medical examination of the victim	S. 164A	S.27	Rule 6	Chapter 4
Medical examination of the accused	S. 53A	No specific guidelines	No specific guidelines	No specific guidelines
Arrest of the accused	S. 41	No specific guidelines	No specific guidelines	No specific guidelines
Collection of forensic evidence		S. 27	Rule 6(6)	No specific provision
Submission of Investigation Report (Chargesheet)	Section 173	No specific provision	No specific provision	No specific provision

and the Model Guidelines for POCSO Act 2012 also provide for additional procedures to be followed in such cases. Table 3.3 gives a summary of the procedural laws for the investigation of cases of sexual offences against children.

Best practices from across the globe

The term best practice in the background of handling of sexual offences against children may be based on the broad parameters of being victim-centric, effective, accountable, and speedy. This section highlights the best practices in some of the jurisdictions across the world compared to the position in India.

1. Standardized Procedures for Law Enforcement for collection of evidence, examination, and interview with the victims by Sexual Assault Response Team (SART)[34]

California law enforcement has developed highly standardized procedures for the collection and preservation of evidence following rapes and other sex crimes and crime scene investigations. The state of California has created an interdisciplinary team known as the Sexual Assault Response Team (SART) that consists of police officers, victim advocates/counsellors, healthcare professionals (forensic examiners), lawyers, and members of other community resource agencies in order to meet the health-related and psychological needs of the vulnerable victim as well as the forensic demands of the justice system. When victims of sexual assault seek medical and legal help, a SART aims to lessen their trauma. A SART aims to promote efficient evidence gathering and preservation during the investigative process and decrease the number of times the victim is questioned. A team approach promotes recovery by assisting the needs of the victim and increasing the possibility that the victim may seek out follow-up assistance.

Procedure followed by SART on receiving the complaint of sexual abuse

A SART is designed to provide victims of sexual assault and the people who care about them with a smooth, coordinated, victim-centred response. A SART gives first responders a place to

- build relationships;
- comprehend their own roles and responsibilities;
- increase the community safety for the victim;
- improved rates of reporting of sexual assault and stalking;
- increase arrests and hold the arrestees accountable;
- sharing of information and resources available;
- identify the gaps in the care delivery system; and
- raise alertness of sexual abuse issues in the community.

Irrespective of the fact who the aggrieved victim first contacts, the SARTs have a standardized procedure to be followed that alarms other members of the team, depending on the victim's requirements.

a) If the victim has granted permission for assistance, a victim advocate is contacted as soon as possible after the sexual assault, irrespective of whether the victim decides to inform about the incident to law authorities.

b) The care of a victim is regarded as a medical emergency at any licenced medical facility. Law enforcement is alerted right away to start the investigation when a victim of sexual assault visits the emergency room and decides to report the incident.

c) The Emergency Department personnel or a Sexual Assault Nurse Examiner (SANE, a nurse specifically trained to gather forensic evidence) is summoned to do the forensic medical examination. In addition, regardless of how much time has passed after the sexual attack, a medical evaluation is advised in every case of sexual assault.

d) The members of the SART group can coordinate in interrogation and cut down on repetition with the advocate on hand to help. With the victim's consent, the advocate may stay in the examination space to assist them. While gathering evidence, the police officer waits outside the examination room. The sexual assault evidence collection kit is either given to the police or placed in a safe place for eventual retrieval.

e) Following the examination, the worker helps the victim to decide for any necessary additional medical treatment. The advocate makes plans to get in touch with the victim for therapeutic counselling and legal representation. The victim and/or victim advocate and law enforcement coordinate to set up a second, in-depth interview wherever necessary.

f) The victim should still undergo a forensic medical examination even if she decides not to contact the police, and the pursuing medical professional ought to forward the sex crime evidence collection kit to Marshall University Forensic Science Centre (MUFSC) so that it will be preserved for potential use in the future. The evidence can last forever if it is gathered and dried correctly.

Trained child forensic interviewers

There has been an increasing acknowledgement of the talent and compassion required to conduct interviews in a friendly manner, yet they may be effectively used as evidence. Ineffective interviewing can alienate and disturb youngsters, provide erroneous judgements of the claims, and give defence lawyers the chance to criticize interviews as suggestive and deceiving.[35] Many jurisdictions in the United States use specialized interviewers because of their experience with children and training in child forensic interviewing.[36] However, it is probable that a large number of police and child protection investigators who speak with kids still lack this training. In a situation of suspected child abuse, the goal of a forensic interview is to extract much trustworthy information as possible from the kid to assist in assessing whether abuse occurred while minimizing the child's trauma while considering any plausible denials of the accusations.[37]

In India, Chapter 3 of the Model Guidelines for POCSO 2012 speaks about Guidelines on interviewing a child: Forensic Interview Protocol. It addresses the fact that the interview stage of the assessment tries to gather evidence directly connected to the claimed incident, like the specifics of the assault, including the time and location, frequency, description of the dresses worn, and so on. This extends beyond the medical history. Interviewing the children is a specialized skill and the model guideline provides that, if possible, such interviewing should be conducted by a trained professional. It also lays down some specific procedures to be considered while organizing the interviews to guarantee that the interaction process does not distress the victim.

In practice, while there are no special child forensic interviewers in India, the investigating officers are the ones conducting interviews of child victims. Time and again, regular training programmes are conducted for the police officers who tackle the cases of CSA so as to sensitize the first responders to the crime of sexual offence against children.

3.   Mandatory reporting of offences

According to the California Child Abuse and Neglect Reporting Act, some professions (referred to as "mandated reporters"), such as teachers and medical staff, are obligated to notify child welfare or law enforcement when they are aware of or have a suspicion of child abuse. The initial child abuse reporting law in California, established in 1963, only applied to doctors.[38] They were under an obligation to reveal any signs of physical abuse they came across a victim. Later, it became apparent that other professionals would also be able to recognize mistreatment as they could be familiar with the concept of child abuse developed throughout time. As a result, the state legislation now has identified a lot more professional bodies as mandatory reporters. Along with the increase in required reporters, the definition of reportable maltreatment was widened to include sexual abuse, emotional maltreatment, and neglect.

In 1980 the Child Abuse and Neglect Reporting Act (CANRA) was promulgated. There have been several changes throughout the years to the idea of child abuse and who is required to report it. The reporting procedures have also been made simpler. In California, several identified professionals are required to report any known or suspected child abuse. Even though it is not required by law, other citizens may report as well. It is crucial for the required reporters to be up to date with the ongoing legal changes. Under CANRA, the legally mandated reporters include the following:

- Any custodian of a clergy member's records
- Child care providers
- Law enforcement officers
- Professionals in the healthcare sector
- Mental healthcare professionals
- Industrial printers for photography and film

The exhaustive list of who have been identified as mandatory reporters is provided in Section 11165.7 of the California Penal Code (PC).

The Model Guidelines under Section 39 POCSO explains the objective of mandatory reporting,[39] which states that without detection, reporting and intervention, these children may remain victims for the rest of their lives, carrying the scars of the abuse throughout their lives and even, in some cases, repeating the pattern of abuse with their own children.

Therefore, the POCSO Act lays the responsibility to report to any offence that one may come across because

> ...*the nature of sexual abuse, the shame that the child victim feels and the possible involvement of a parent, family friend or other close person, makes it extremely detrimental.* (emphasis added)[40]

There has been an obligation on the media, studio, and photographic facilities under S. 20 of the Act to report the matter to the law enforcement authorities if they come across any sexually exploitative material involving a child. And at the same time any person including a child having an apprehension of the commission of an offence under the Act or knowledge that an offence has been committed under the Act is obligated to report such offences. However, in the absence of identification of specific mandatory reporters under the POCSO Act or Rule, this provision may remain as a dead letter of the law until there is routine orientation and awareness-building of the members of the community at large, regarding what constituted sexual offences and what are the physical and mental signs that the prospective reporters should look for in children to find out possible abuse on such children.

Among the nations with a particular provision pertaining to obligatory reporting as a step taken to prevent and reduce child abuse are the United States of America, Canada, Australia, and India.[41] In Australia, the liability for mandatorily reporting of an offence has been imposed on all citizens in some jurisdictions and the police, teachers, doctors, and nurses in almost all jurisdictions.[42]

4.   Victim receiving centres and advocacy and support programmes

For young victims and their families, court cases are distressing. The process's combative character, lengthy procedures, and repeated delays can all be scary. Professionals are also concerned that children's exposure to the accused in court and their testimony about painful, personal victimization experiences might cause them to undergo secondary trauma.[43]

Child Abuse Services Team (CAST) is a one-stop receiving and support centre for child abuse victims at Orange County, CA, that opened in 1989 to *reduce the trauma for child victims during the investigation of their abuse.* Most of CAST's clients are sexual assault victims; however, some are victims of domestic abuse, homicide, kidnapping, etc. Social workers, physicians, a nurse, a deputy attorney, a therapist, child advocates, and a representative from Victim Witness are all involved in the interdisciplinary, public/private CAST project. All the law enforcement units in Orange County refer their children to CAST for forensic interviews, medical examinations, crisis inter-ference treatment, and victim advocacy by volunteer Child Advocates. This facility's main goal is to stabilize the child victim's physical and mental state before preparing him or her for the criminal court system.

Advocacy for Victims of Crime by the Canadian Resource Centre for Victims of Crime (CRCVC) assists victims in a number of ways, such as by outlining the criminal justice system, providing resources and research, providing emotional support, making recommendations to other organizations that may be able to help, and assisting victims in locating the information they require. The CRCVC is a non-profit, national organization that advocates for the rights of victims and efficient judicial reform. All over Canada, the CRCVC offers services to victims. The CRCVC was established in 1993 by the Canadian Police Association and has assisted hundreds of crime victims.[44]

In India non-governmental organizations (NGOs) play a poignant role in providing support to victims of crime. For example, an NGO working specially for child victims is Council to Secure Justice that supports victims who are sexually abused so they can pursue justice for the wrong committed to them. In the course of criminal procedures, they offer survivors legal and psychological help. They offer victim attorneys to help public prosecutors in sexual injury cases, either directly or through pro bono networks. Lawyers fight against bail, help survivors tell their stories in court, and push for quick trials and accurate verdicts. The social workers help children and their families at police stations, hospitals, Child Welfare Committee meetings, and courtrooms as they navigate the criminal justice system together. They keep the family and kid informed of developments in their case and provide information to the court and kid Welfare Committee so that decisions are made that are in the best interest of the child.

After the Indira Gandhi Matritva Sahyog Yojna (IGMSY) was terminated on March 31, 2017, the Ministry of Women and Child Development (MWCD) in India brought the "SAKHI" programme, which is a federally sponsored initiative funded by the Nirbhaya Fund and designed to provide support for distressed women who have experienced violence in their homes, community, and workplace. At these One Stop Centres (OSCs), specialized assistance is offered to aggrieved women of all ages who are the victims of sexual harassment, domestic violence, sexual assault, acid assaults, honour-related violence, human trafficking, or witch-hunting. These facilities are intended to offer shelter, video conferencing capabilities, medical assistance, help with filing a complaint with the police, emotional support and counselling, legal aid, and emergency response and rescue services.[45]

The services provided by the One-Stop Sakhi Centres can be enumerated as follows (Figure 3.2).

When it comes to the functioning of OSCs in the states of Odisha, Jharkhand, and West Bengal, Odisha and Jharkhand have functional OSCs for every district as opposed to WB where the functioning of OSCs is non-existent.[46]

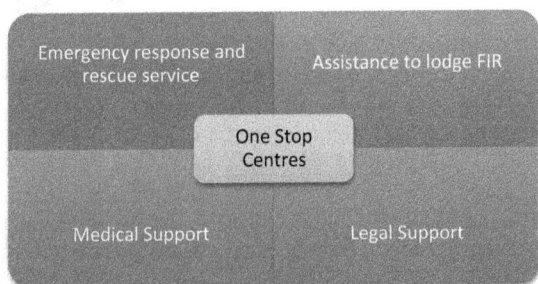

Figure 3.2 Number of cases reported in the sample states under the POCSO Act.

Conclusion

The role of police as the first stakeholder to start the criminal justice process in motion in all cases cannot be undermined, and it is more significant in cases of sexual offences against children, as they have to play the dual role first as a sensitized and sympathetic counsellor and second as an investigating officer. Therefore, as first responders it is imperative that the police should be perceived by the members of society as approachable and eager to take their information seriously enough to start the investigation. This will give the victims and their families enough confidence to report the crime to the police. When it comes to sexual offences, whether against adults or children in the Indian society, there are great opposing forces acting against reporting of such crimes in forms of taboos surrounding sex and sexual acts generally and stigma and victim shaming specifically. The response and approach of police towards the victim and their cases require effective implementation of the law especially of the victim-friendly procedures.

The major steps involved in dealing with a CSA case by the police include registering the information; recording the statement of the victims; medical examination; search and seizure of material evidence, including forensic evidence like (semen, hair, nail, blood, etc.); storing and sending the forensic samples to the forensic laboratories for analysis; arrest of the accused person; and recording of statements of witnesses including the victim by the Magistrate; we find that in most of these steps the victim's involvement is quite prominent. Therefore, the success of the investigation largely depends on the interest, cooperation, and confidence of the victims on the police and their processes.

For the first time ever, the POCSO Act introduces the concept of mandatory reporting in child sexual abuse cases; however, the data collected from the three shows a no implementation of such provisions. Therefore, unless awareness campaigns are conducted in accordance with Section 43 of the

POCSO Act, 2012, which mandates that the Central Government and every State Government will take all means to provide broad exposure to the provisions of the Act, such provisions will only exist on paper.

There have to be more coordinated efforts from not only the stakeholders like the Government or police but also civil society members in bringing awareness about CSA and the POCSO Act. The Police play the most crucial role and there should be efforts with the support of OSCs and NGOs to put the child through minimum procedural harassment and stabilize him/her. Also all-concerted effort to standardize protocol to report, handle victims, and investigation of CSA must be in place. Effective forensic training for Police, medical practitioners, and nurses should be made mandatory. Such efforts will not only give confidence to the victims and the family but also spell out effective criminal justice administration under the POCSO Act.

Notes

1　Anviti Chaturvedi, *Police Reforms in India: An Analytical Study*, 6 (2017), available at chrome-extension://efaidnbmnnnibpcajpcglclefindmkaj/https://crcvc.ca/wp -content/uploads/2021/09/advocacy.pdf
2　Pulkit Taneja, "Policing Reforms in India." *International Journal of Legal Science and Innovation*, 3 (2021): 865–874.
3　Chattoraj, P. (2013). Chapter 4: PREVALENCE OF RAPE and EVOLUTION OF RAPE LAWS IN INDIA -Bridging the Gap between "Is" and "Ought." https://library.kiit.ac.in/digital-library/
4　Anil Redhy, "Functions, Roles and Duties of Police in General." *Draft Police Man. BPRD*, 2 (2018): 1–504.
5　Ibid.
6　Manish Kaithwas and Neena Pandey, "Incompetency and Challenges of Police in Rape Cases." *Social Work Chronicle*, 7 (2018): 51–70, available at https://search .proquest.com/docview/2087202296?accountid=13828%0Ahttp://find.shef.ac.uk /openurl/44SFD/44SFD_services_page?url_ver=Z39.88-2004&rft_val_fmt=info :ofi/fmt:kev:mtx:journal&genre=article&sid=ProQ:ProQ%3Asciencejournals &atitle=Incompetency+and+Ch
7　Vik et al., "Is Police Investigation of Rape Biased by Characteristics of Victims?," 98–106.
8　David J. Hansen and Kathryn R. Wilson, "Child Sexual Abuse." *Encyclopedia of Psychology & Law* (2007), available at https://www.researchgate.net/publication /228599035_Child_Sexual_Abuse
9　Paromita Chattoraj, "Response to the Offence of Rape by the Criminal Justice System -An Empirical Study in the States of Odisha, Jharkhand and West Bengal," 2020. ICSSR, New Delhi.- F. No. G-35/2017-18/ICSSR/RP
10　Patrick Tidmarsh, Stephanie Sharman and Gemma Hamilton, "Police Officers Perception of Specialised Training, Skills and Qualities Required to Investigate Sexual Crime." *Police Practice and Research*, 22 (2021): 475–490.
　　Danielle Ostrander, "Police Perceptions on False Accusations of Sexual Assault" (Electronic Theses and Dissertations, Paper 3428, 2018), available at https://dc.etsu.edu/etd/3428%0Ahttps://dc.etsu.edu/etd/3428/
11　Emma Sleath and Ray Bull, "Police Perceptions of Rape Victims and the Impact on Case Decision Making: A Systematic Review." *Aggression and Violent Behavior*, 34 (2017): 102–112.

12 G.S. Bajpai and Raghav Mendiratta, "Gender Notions in Judgments of Rape Cases." *Journal of the Indian Law Institute*, 60 (2018): 298–311, https://www.jstor.org/stable/10.2307/26826643

13 Friederike Eyssel and Gerd Bohner, "Schema Effects of Rape Myth Acceptance on Judgments of Guilt and Blame in Rape Cases: The Role of Perceived Entitlement to Judge." *Journal of Interpersonal Violence*, 26 (2011): 1579–1605.

14 Tidmarsh, Sharman and Hamilton, *supra* note 10.

15 Christine Eastwood, "Child Sexual Abuse and the Criminal Justice System." *Australia and New Zealand Journal of Law and Education*, 8 (2003): 111–125, available at https://www.researchgate.net/publication/27477770_Child_sexual_abuse_and_the_criminal_justice_system_What_educators_need_to_know

16 Jan Jordan, "Perfect Victims, Perfect Policing? Improving Rape Complainants' Experiences of Police Investigations." *Public Administration*, 86 (2008): 699–719.

17 Partners in Law and Development, "Towards Victim Friendly Responses and Procedures for Prosecuting Rape" (2015), available at https://doj.gov.in/sites/default/files/PLD report.pdf

18 Emmanouil I. Sakelliadis, Chara A. Spiliopoulou and Stavroula A. Papadodima, "Forensic Investigation of Child Victim with Sexual Abuse." *Indian Pediatrics*, 46 (2009): 144–151, available at https://d1wqtxts1xzle7.cloudfront.net/69226519/Forensic_investigation_of_child_victim_w20210908-30916-17ybs9w.pdf?1631161510=&response-content-disposition=inline%3B+filename%3DForensic_investigation_of_child_victim_w.pdf&Expires=1643985603&Signature=NHiYP

19 Rebecca Campbell et al., "Systems Change Analysis of SANE Programs: Identifying the Mediating Mechanisms of Criminal Justice System Impact" (2008), available at https://www.ncjrs.gov/pdffiles1/nij/grants/226497.pdf

20 Press Information Bureau Government of India, "Sakhi Centres" (2016).

21 Prachi Sharma, M.K. Unnikrishnan and Abhishek Sharma, "Sexual Violence in India: Addressing Gaps between Policy and Implementation." *Health Policy Plan*, 30 (2015): 656–659.

22 Jaiswal Hrishikesh, "Indian Legal Position on Child Sexual Abuse: A Brief Analysis Analysis of Indian Criminal Law and Its Comparison with Laws of Other Nations." *Legal Service India*, (2019): 1–13.

23 Cognizable offences are those offences in which the police can arrest the accused without warrant. On the other hand non-cognizable offences are those in which the police have no authority to arrest without warrant. These are offences that lack urgency and therefore time is available to get the warrant from the magistrate.

24 National Crime Records Bureau, "Police Disposal of Crime against Women Cases (State / UT-wise)- Crime in India." https://ncrb.gov.in/en/crime-in-india.

25 Crl. Appeal 1874 of 2022.

26 C.A 5802/2022.

27 Wendy A. Walsh et al., "Which Sexual Abuse Victims Receive a Forensic Medical Examination?. The Impact of Children's Advocacy Centers." *Child Abuse & Neglect*, 31 (2007): 1053–1068.

28 Tanya Smith et al., "The Medical Evaluation of Prepubertal Children with Suspected Sexual Abuse." *Paediatrics & Child Health*, 25 (2020): 180–186.

29 Bernd Herrmann et al., "Physical Examination in Child Sexual Abuse - Approaches and Current Evidence." *Deutsches Ärzteblatt international*, 111 (2014): 692–703.

30 Bhosale Minakshi, Caryn Carvalho and Nazrah Shaikh, "Child Sexual Abuse: Level of Awareness among Medical Students in context of the POCSO Act." *Journal of Medical Science and Clinical Research*, 6 (2018): 400–406, available at https://www.researchgate.net/profile/Minakshi_Bhosale3/publication/327644784_Child_Sexual_Abuse_Level_of_Awareness_among_Medical_Students_in_context_of_the_POCSO_Act/links/5b9b4f6da6fdccd3cb533729/Child-Sexual-Abuse-Level-of-Awareness-among-Medical-Studen

31 Shubhi Mack and Ishita Chatterjee, "Role of Forensic Evidence in Criminal Justice Delivery System in India." *Natural Volatiles and Essential Oils*, 8 (2021): 5765–5770.

32 Gajendra Kumar Goswamy, "Role of Forensics in Strengthening Child Rights under the POCSO Act 2012" (2020). https://doi.org/10.13140/RG.2.2.14951.06569 Thesis submitted for Doctor of Sciences to National Forensic Science University, Gandhinagar.

33 A. Badiye, N. Kapoor and R.G. Menezes, "Chain of Custody," in *StatPearls* [Internet] (Treasure Island: StatPearls Publishing, February 17, 2022), 2022 January–. PMID: 31869141.

34 West Virginia Bureau for Public Health, Health Statistics Center, *Behavioral Risk Factor Surveillance System Survey* (Charleston: Department of Health and Human Resources, 2008). See www.wvdhhr.org/bph/hsc/.

35 Lindsay E. Cronch, Jodi L. Viljoen and David J. Hansen, "Forensic Interviewing in Child Sexual Abuse Cases: Current Techniques and Future Directions." *Aggression and Violent Behavior* 11 (2006): 195–207.

36 Chris Newlin et al., "Child Forensic Interviewing: Best Practices." *Juvenile Justice Bulletin* (2015), available at http://www.ojjdp.gov/pubs/248749.pdf

37 APSAC Taskforce, "Forensic Interviewing in Cases of Suspected Child Abuse." *The American Professional Society on the Abuse of Children* (APSAC) (2012), available at https://www.apsac.org/guidelines%0AAPSAC

38 Child Abuse & Prevention Council, "Child Abuse Reporting Guidelines- Child Abuse Prevention Council- County of Santa Clara" (1998), available at https://capc .sccgov.org/child-abuse-reporting-guidelines

39 Section 39 POCSO Act – Guidelines for child to take assistance of experts, etc.

40 Centre for Child and the Law, National Law School of India University, Bangalore, An Analysis of Mandatory Reporting under the POCSO Act and its Implications on the Rights of Children.

41 Norazla Abdul Wahab, "Mandatory Reporting As a Mechanism of Preventing Child Sexual Abuse Cases," in *Proceeding – 3rd Putrajaya International Conference on Children, Women, Elderly and Disabled People (PICCWED 3), 28–29 October 2017.* Hotel Bangi-Putrajaya, Bandar Baru Bangi, Malaysia, 2017, available at https://www.researchgate.net/publication/320799408%0AMANDATORY

42 Ben Mathews, "Mandatory Reporting Laws and Identification of Child Abuse and Neglect: Consideration of Differential Maltreatment Types, and a Cross-Jurisdictional Analysis of Child Sexual Abuse Reports." *Social Science*, 3 (2014): 460–482.

43 Helen Stalford, Liam Cairns and Jeremy Marshall, "Achieving Child Friendly Justice through Child Friendly Methods: Let's Start with the Right to Information." *Social Inclusion*, 5 (2017): 207–218, available at https://www.researchgate.net/pub-lication/320048036_Achieving_Child_Friendly_Justice_through_Child_Friendly _Methods_Let's_Start_with_the_Right_to_Information/link/59cb2139a6fdcc451 d582f0b/download

44 Advocacy for Victims of Crime, 1983.

45 Goswamy, *supra* note 35.

46 Press Information Bureau Government of India, *supra* note 23.

4 Dynamics of trial process in Child Sexual Offence Cases

Introduction

The POCSO Act apart from being a stringent penal law is also meant to be a piece of social welfare legislation aiming to provide justice to the child victim. The vulnerability associated with the victims of sexual abuse makes it important for the stakeholders to handle the cases in a sensitive manner, safeguarding their special needs through the trajectory of the criminal justice process.[1] There is a constant need to build a comforting environment also in the court for child victims and ensure consistent availability of support.[2] The trial of POCSO cases should consider the intricacies of abuse and make the child victim feel supported during taking of testimony of the child, evidence being sensitively valued and throughout maintaining the privacy of the child.[3] These pro-victim provisions could go a long way in improving the otherwise declining conviction rate in CSA cases.[4] Pacifying the ordeal of sexual offences for the victim is as vital as trying the guilty.[5] However, for the justice system to work effectively to punish the guilty, sensitization of various organs involved is of utmost importance.[6]

Concept of Special Courts

Special Courts, i.e., the courts that have been sanctioned to oversee only one type of cases, are a widely sought-after answer for the Indian courts in dealing with special categories of cases based on either the nature of the offence, public interest, or national security or vulnerability of the victim. Such courts are often invoked to fasten the rate of disposal of such cases they have been allotted to decide and help to reduce the overall pendency rate of such cases. Also, regular courts lack the infrastructure which is required under certain laws such as the Protection of Children from Sexual Offences Act, 2012 (POCSO).

The POCSO Act 2012 speaks for the establishment of Special Courts under Chapter VII Section 28 of the Act[7] for the purpose of ensuring speedy trial. It is the responsibility of the state to designate a Court of Sessions in each district as the Special Court after consulting the Chief Justice of the High Court. The special attribute of Special Courts lies in the way trial proceedings

DOI: 10.4324/9781003345244-4

are conceived to be conducted. They are to ensure that the trial is conducted in a victim-friendly manner where the statement of the victim is recorded either "in-camera" (i.e. in the absence of any third party), via audio-video means, or behind curtains or screens that separate the victim and the accused, which is intended to protect the identity of the child as well as prevents her from being re-traumatized. The Special Court is mandated to incorporate steps and procedures for making the recording of evidence and trial of offences more child-friendly.

The POCSO Act mentions about very inadequate physical requisites for the functioning of Special Courts. The primary requisites include the designating of courts to function as Special Courts, appointing prosecutors as the Special Public Prosecutors (SPP)[8] and to take enough measures to prevent the contact between the accused and the victim and during the recording of evidence.[9] Though the Act lays down the responsibility on the Special Courts to ensure that child-friendly atmosphere is maintained, it does not elaborate on the meaning and the definition or the structural modifications required for making an atmosphere "child-friendly."[10]

A study by the Vidhi Centre for Legal Policy[11] on the working of Special Courts in legislation between 1950 and 2015 revealed that the laws and regulations have the tendency to use the terms *set up* or *designate* interchangeably with Special Courts, despite the fact that these two terms have different meanings. While setting up a court implicated making a new court with new infrastructure and specially dedicated staff, designating a court meant allocation of an additional caseload of independent categories to a judge who still is responsible for their regular load.[12] The goals of Special Courts have been hampered by the unclear and uneven formation of Special Courts and the propensity to *designate* rather than build new infrastructure.[13] In 2019, the Supreme Court ordered the establishment of a centrally funded specialized court in each district of the nation with more than 100 POCSO Act FIRs to handle matters of sexual crimes against children only.[14] However, more than three years have passed since the Supreme Court's ruling, and many districts across the nation still lack such courts.[15]

It is pertinent to mention that regarding the duration for the completion of the trial of sexual offence cases, the general law under s.309 CrPC provides the period of 2 months that was introduced in the 2018 Criminal Law Amendment; however, the special law u/s 35 of the POCSO Act remains unchanged and provides that the trial of CSA cases to be completed within 1 year from taking cognizance of the offence. Despite the POCSO Act, the duration of the trial in 69% of cases disposed of by POCSO courts in 2019 was between 1 and 10 years.[16] As per the Crime in India statistics 2021 released by the National Crime Records Bureau (NCRB), 92.9% of POCSO cases in Special Courts are pending. According to the 2018 data from the NCRB, 78% of trials in fast track were completed over a year, 42% were completed after a period of more than three years, and 17% more than five years' time.[17]

The general consensus is that the Special Courts have not been able to achieve their desired objectives, and several factors may be held responsible for failing the purpose behind the establishment of such courts. In reality, Special Courts have the same, if not greater, issues than normal courts because they are often named rather than established.[18] Judges who are already overworked are given additional categories of cases to handle on top of their current workload without any extra resources or assistance. In this situation, the overall case disposal rate would decrease.[19] Additionally, quicker case disposal cannot be anticipated without easing procedural restrictions or streamlining Special Courts.[20]

Right to speedy trial is not just a right for the accused, but it is more so, for the victim, who waits to see that justice is done for the wrong done. If we consider the statistics of the National Crime Records Bureau during the years 2014–2021, the pendency of POCSO cases is seen to be constantly on a rise with an average pendency rate of 91.8% for these eight years. The highest pendency rate was 94.7% in the year 2020. Pendency of POCSO cases like other cases is definitely a pain point; however, there is also another side to the coin where we find an over-zealous attitude of the courts in trying the cases with "ugly haste." For instance, in the case of Raj Kumar Yadav vs. The State of Bihar[21] on the very day of framing of the charge, the accused received the police papers, and the entire trial was concluded on the very same day. Thereafter, a division bench of Patna High Court observed that

> *because of the blatant violation of the principles of natural justice and total disregard to the mandatory statutory provisions of the CrPC, the impugned judgement cannot be sustained, rather the trial itself is vitiated. The manner in which the trial had begun, continued, and came to an end by the learned Court simply shows the glaring maltreatment of the prescribed law for conducting a trial and, accordingly, there is no other option except to direct for de-novo trial of the accused from the stage for framing of charge.*

The bench also referred to the cases of *Md. Major @ Mejar vs. State of Bihar*[22] and *Anokhilal vs State of Madhya Pradesh*[23] wherein it was held that:

> Speedy trial is undoubtedly required in criminal matters and that would be a part of the guarantee of fair trial. However, attempts to expedite the process should not be at the expense of the basic elements of fairness to the accused, which is the primary postulate of the criminal justice administration system. In the pursuit for expeditious disposal of cases, the cause of justice must never be allowed to suffer or be sacrificed. What is paramount is the cause of justice and keeping the basic ingredients which secure that as a core idea and ideal, the process may be expedited, but fast tracking of process must never ever result in burying the cause of justice.

Case study

In the three states of Odisha, Jharkhand, and West Bengal Special Courts designated to try specifically the cases of CSA were functional. They were not exclusive courts to try POCSO cases, but merely Sessions Courts (courts to try criminal Matters at the district level) designated as Special Courts under the POCSO Act.

Role of the Judge under the POCSO Act

The adversarial system of criminal justice administration envisages the judge as an impartial arbitrator: the one who decides which way the truth lies, after a clash of adversaries, and out of the dialectical contest between the prosecutor and the defence – the truth is supposed to emerge. But speaking of a Judge's role under the POCSO Act, there are some additional responsibilities on the Judge of a Special Court hearing a case of sexual offence against children under the POCSO Act, which is to ensure child-friendly atmosphere during the trial. Section 25 of the POCSO Act[24] mandates the responsibility of the Magistrate to ensure that the child victim's statement is recorded as is deposed by the child victim. Section 26 of the POCSO Act[25] mentions some procedural safeguards to be ensured by the Judge in the course of trial, viz., the presence of guardians wherever necessary; the assistance of the interpreter shall be taken by the Magistrate; and wherever possible, the Magistrate shall record the statement using audio-video means. Section 33 further reiterates that the Special Court to conduct the trial permitting breaks at regular intervals to the child victim during the trial, ensuring that the defence lawyers do not intimidate the child victim etc., thereby creating a child-friendly atmosphere while trying a case under the POCSO Act.[26]

Case study

From the cross-sectional study conducted in WB, OD, and JH, it was observed that in most of the cases in the three states, the Judges ensured the presence of a guardian during the trial. In the case of a girl child victim, the Judge usually asked the mother to stay. But the ultimate choice as to who shall accompany the victim remained with the victim herself or himself. From the responses of the judges interviewed, the mandates mentioned u/s 33 of the POCSO Act are followed and most of the judges allowed frequent breaks to the child victim wherever necessary. The judges also ensured that the enquiries of the lawyers to the child victim are put through the Special Judge. The Judges prefer conducting in-camera trials to protect the child's identity and also to make the child victim feel comfortable.

Duration for victim's deposition

Section 35(1) of the POCSO Act mentions that the child's testimony is to be recorded by the Special Court within one month of taking cognizance of the offence and also record the reasons for the delay, if any. The Bombay High Court in the case of Atul Gorakhnath Ambale vs. The State of Maharashtra,[27] observed that

> *"it is imperative to record at least the evidence of the child victim, as soon as possible, lest the victim forgets the incident due to passage of time or on account of counselling. Early on, the kid or victim would be able to recall the incident clearly, as it happened, and identify the offender. In fact, it would be advantageous to the accused if the child/victim was checked after a couple of years. The accused's appearance could alter slightly, making it challenging for the child or victim to identify or recognise the offender. The child/victim may be from another State and may also desire to return to his/her hometown, which is also a possibility."* In this light, the Court issued the following orders to all the Special Courts in Maharashtra:

1. ensuring that the statement of the child victim is recorded and registered as soon as possible,
2. to swiftly complete the recording of the evidence, including the victim's cross-examination and main examination,
3. to prevent the victim/child from being summoned to court regularly, since this would exacerbate their suffering,
4. to prevent postponements when examining the victim; and if permitted, the reasons to be noted,

5.   child-friendly procedures to be used to make sure the child/victim is safe, at ease, and not in any way exposed to the accused, and
6.   to ensure that the child's parents or any other adult with whom the child has confidence is present when they are being examined.

Case study

The data from the study reveals that in the states of Odisha (62.5%) and Jharkhand (50%), most of the Judges admitted to the fact that they take the deposition of the child victim within 30 days of taking cognizance of the matter. The majority of the Judges in West Bengal (70%) admitted to have recorded the evidence of the child victim after 30 days of taking cognizance of the matter.

It is interesting to note that the Special Courts in the three states are designated Special Courts and not newly set-up courts to try POCSO cases only, and the Judges are often overburdened with other case matters too. This happened to be one of the primary reasons why there was a delay in taking the evidence of the child victim in the three states. In addition to this, the reluctance of the victim's family to cooperate with the process and the adverse condition (physical and or emotional) of the child victim also contributed to the delay caused in recording the statement of the child by the Judges.

Pendency of cases

According to the latest report of National Crime Records Bureau's Crime in India statistics (2021) the pendency rate in POCSO cases is 92.9%. The average time taken to dispose of a POCSO case is 509 days.[28] The POCSO Act under s. 35 provides for 1 years' time from the date of taking cognizance, and Sec. 309 CrPC[29] provides a period of two months (section 309 CrPC) from the date of filing of chargesheet, to complete the trial.

The Committee on Reforms of Criminal Justice System Government of India, Ministry of Home Affairs (commonly known as the Malimath Committee report) in 2003 stated:

It is common knowledge that the two major problems besieging the Criminal Justice System are huge pendency of criminal cases and the inordinate delay in disposal of criminal cases on the one hand and the very low rate of conviction in cases involving serious crimes on the other. This has encouraged crime. Violent and organized crimes have become the order of the day. As chances of convictions are remote, crime has at the two major problems besieging the Criminal Justice System are huge pendency of criminal cases and the inordinate delay in disposal of criminal cases on the one hand and the very low rate of conviction in cases involving serious crimes on the other. (emphasis added)

It is pertinent to mention that the new Bhartiya Nagarik Suraksha Sanhita Bill 2023 (BNSS), which is proposed to replace the CrPC to mitigate the delay in trial procedure, provides for specified timelines that include viz.: (i) giving judgement within 30 days of completion of arguments (extendable up to 60 days), (ii) informing the victim of progress of investigation within 90 days, and (iii) framing of charges by a sessions court within 60 days from the first hearing on such charges.

Case study

The average length of a trial of child sexual abuse cases in the states of Odisha, Jharkhand, and West Bengal ranges anywhere between six months to more than a year in certain cases, as revealed by the field study. Frequent adjournments by the advocates and the caseload on the judges make it difficult for the judges to complete the trial within the stipulated time period.

According to the responses collected from the Judges, the maximum delay occurred in the stage of examination of prosecution witnesses.

Admissibility of forensic evidence

Forensic evidence

Section 3 of the Indian Evidence Act, 1872, defines the term evidence, which states to mean and include an oral and documentary evidence.[30] Under the law, there are many different types of evidence, with "material evidence" being the most significant. It is typically found at the crime site or in a location where the accused or victim was present before or after the incident. Blood, hair, semen, fingerprints, shoeprints, and other forensic evidence are all important sources of information that might help identify the perpetrator of a crime. In sexual offence cases, the forensic reports are prepared by scientists or criminalists who analyse the forensic samples (semen, nails, hairs, etc.) and prepare the reports. Judges and solicitors, who both have little to no background in science and technology, have found it difficult to accept scientific findings.[31]

The material (scientific) evidence is taken as relevant and admissible evidence u/s 45 of the Indian Evidence Act, 1872. However, a written report as an expert's opinion is considered as weak and not credible evidence and many a time to understand such a report the expert is involved as a witness for giving oral testimony. But in spite of such expert testimony, courts are reluctant to base a conviction only on such testimony of the expert explaining the scientific report, unless it is corroborated by other independent evidence.[32] Once the court accepts an expert's view, it becomes the court's opinion instead of the expert's.[33] Bentham argued that witnesses serve as the legal system's *eyes and ears*. As held in State of UP v. Hari Chand,[34] "it would be incorrect on the part of the court to accept the medical evidence and disregard the eye witness' testimony if the ocular evidence provided by the witness differed with the medical evidence (expert's opinion)."[35]

The primary reason for placing less reliance on forensic evidence in sexual offence cases is due to the fact that the collection and handling of forensic samples by the police is not standardized in India. Samples are stored at places without proper hygiene, and refrigeration and transportation to forensic labs are done without following a proper chain of custody.

Forensic samples

In case of sexual offences, forensic samples are collected by way of medical examination of the accused person u/s 53A CrPC and of the victim u/s 164A CrPC. There are no standard procedures that are followed by the Investigating Officer for the collection, storage, and transport of such samples to the forensic labs. Although the Central Forensic Science Laboratory Directorate of Forensic Sciences Services has provided for guidelines for Investigating Officers for collecting, storing, and transporting the biological samples collected from the crime scene, these are not consistently or uniformly followed by the police because they cannot be enforced if not followed.[36] At the moment, there are no regulations governing the use of DNA technology for person identification. Several expert organizations, including the Law Commissions, have already examined how DNA technology is used and regulated.[37] In July 2017, the Commission filed a draught Bill along with its findings.[38] The DNA Technology (Use and Application) Regulation Bill, 2018 was presented in this context on August 9, 2018, in Lok Sabha (lower house of the Parliament) and passed in January 2019 but did not go through Rajya Sabha (upper house of the Parliament) and it lapsed and was finally withdrawn in July 2023, so that aspects regarding DNA data storage, sharing, and privacy could be looked into by the Ministry of Electronics and Information Technology.[39] The Bill was meant to control how DNA technology is used to identify people in both criminal and civil cases. The new BNSS

Bill provides for more flexibility by allowing forensic experts to visit crime scenes to collect forensic evidence and record the process on mobile phones or any other electronic device.

Case study

In India, the collection of forensic evidence is done by medical practitioners who conduct the medical examination of the victim and the accused as the case may be. The samples are then handed over to the Investigating Officer charged with sending them to the laboratory for forensic analysis. Meanwhile, due to the lack of available resources, there may be delay in sending the samples for analysis, which may lead to manhandling and destruction in the quality of samples. The interviews of the Judges conducted in the three states revealed that most of the Judges found forensic evidence to be credible only when it was corroborated by other evidence. This attitude was seen because of the fact that police do not maintain a chain of custody while forwarding the samples for forensic analysis. There were instances where the Judges pointed out that the samples for forensic analysis were being stored in the Malkhana (store room) of the police station without proper refrigeration system which deteriorates the quality of the live samples (usually semen or blood). Such samples when sent for analysis to the Forensic Science Laboratories after inordinate delay lose their value because of such lapse of time. Accordingly, conducting forensic examination of such deteriorated samples yields no results. Therefore, the Judges were reluctant in using the forensic analysis reports as a standalone piece of evidence in sexual offence cases.

Compensation

In a culture where the victim of rape is considered worse than the offender, compensation to the victim of rape is unquestionably crucial for her rehabilitation. Although monetary compensation may not restore the victim emotionally, it definitely allows the victim to use the money for her physical and mental rehabilitation. Section 357 CrPC speaks of providing compensation to the crime victims on account of the convicted person either from the fine amount or compensation paid by the offender in case the fine does not form part of the punishment.[40] Section 357 was incomplete in itself as it did not provide for all the victims of the crime where the trial cannot be concluded, for instance, if the accused has died or escaped or discharged or acquitted due to deficient evidence. In order to close this gap, the legislature added section 357A, which made the State responsible for compensating the victim or any of the dependents for any injury or loss as a result of the crime.[41] One of the major lacuna under Section 357 CrPC was that there was no liability on the State to provide compensation to the victim. Section 357A was a constructive step in resolving the victims' problems as a result. According to this provision, the State is responsible for compensating the victim or any dependents who have suffered because of the crime.

Every State Government in coordination with the Central Government has to prepare a Victim Compensation Scheme (VCS) u/s 357A of the Code.[42] The victim of a crime or his or her dependents will be able to make a claim through this programme for compensation for their loss or harm. The state is required to establish and manage a fund for paying the aforementioned compensation. There are two ways that a victim might profit from victim compensation. First, the District Legal Service Authority (DLSA) or the State Legal Service Authority (SLSA) may be recommended for compensation by the court considering the victim's case. Then, in accordance with the plan in place in their State, the authorities will compensate the sufferer. Second, Section 357(4) permits the victim to apply directly to the DLSA or the SLSA for compensation. Since the 2008 amendment, almost every state has developed its own victim compensation programme. For the offences stated in the plan, this scheme stipulates both the minimum and maximum level of compensation.

The SLSA and DLSA must receive both a physical copy and an electronic copy of the FIR in order for the police to report the offences covered by this scheme. Additionally, it enables SLSA/DLSA to conduct preliminary fact-checking procedures on its own in order to provide victims with interim compensation. Additionally, it has provisions for immediate compensation in worthy circumstances, which may be in the amount of Rs. 5,000–10,000. According to the Central Victim Compensation Fund Scheme Guidelines, it has further enhanced the minimum compensation sum for rape cases. In rape cases, the minimum award is Rs. 4 lakhs, but Rs. 5 lakhs is the minimum award in gang rape cases.[43] Even though we are yet to assess the impact of this scheme, it can nevertheless be said that this is a significant breakthrough for the rehabilitation of female victims in the society.

Compensation to the child victim under POCSO Act and Rules

According to Section 33(8) of the POCSO Act, the Special Courts have the authority to directly pay any compensation that may be prescribed to the child for bodily or mental stress inflicted or for prompt rehabilitation in addition to sentence to the accused. In accordance with Rule 9(1) of the POCSO Rules 2020, the court may also grant interim compensation to satisfy immediate needs, provide relief, or facilitate rehabilitation at any point following the registration of the FIR. Interim compensation is to be deducted from the final compensation awarded in the appropriate cases. In addition, by Rule 9(2) the court is permitted to recommend for compensation whether the accused is found guilty, even acquitted or discharged, or remains untraced or unknown, if the court determines that the victim has suffered loss or injury as a result of the offence (u/s.2 (wa)CrPC). The Special Court is allowed to direct the payment of compensation to the victims under Rule 9(3) of the POCSO Rules 2020.

It is important to refer to the interpretation of the above Rules and Provision by the Hon'ble Delhi High Court in Mst. X (Through Mother and Natural Guardian) v. State & ors[44] which reads thus:

(k) There appears to be some dissonance and confusion insofar as the use of the words "recommendation", "order" and "direction" is concerned, in that sections 357A(2) and (3) CrPC., Clause 9(1)(Part-II) of the Delhi Victim Compensation Scheme 2018 (DVS) and Rule 9(2) of the 2020 Rules speak of the court making "recommendation" for award of compensation to the concerned legal service authority; but Rule 9(1) and (3) of the 2020 Rules say that the court may make an "order" and "direction" for award of interim compensation and compensation respectively. In relation to payment of interim compensation, under Rule 9(1) the court is empowered to make "an order for interim compensation." (italics original)

Therefore, when an application for compensation comes in front of the court, the court may in its discretion do either of the two things: firstly, the court upon an application for interim compensation make an order to the tune of such interim compensation; secondly, if the application is for compensation, the court may make an order to that effect leaving the amount to be decided by the concerned legal service authority under the applicable schedule of the District Victim Compensation Scheme (DVCS) 2018.

But contrary to the above, in another case in *Mother Minor Victim No. 1 & 2 v. State and Others*[45] the Delhi High Court held that,

It is well settled that every statutory power is also coupled with the duty to exercise it. In view of the express provisions of Section 33(8) of the

POCSO Act and Rule 7 of the said Rules (Rule 9 POCSO Rules, 2020 as is currently in force), the duty to award compensation in appropriate cases has been conferred on the Special Court and therefore, it is incumbent on the Special Court to pass necessary orders for compensation/interim compensation without delegating the said power and direct the concerned Legal Services Authority to examine any claim for compensation payable to a minor victim under the POCSO Act. (emphasis original)

In *Nipun Saxena v. Union of India*,[46] the Supreme Court ordered the National Legal Services Authority (NALSA) to create the Model Rules for Victim Compensation for Sexual Offences and Acid Attacks in order to eliminate the differences between the victim compensation programmes of various states and UTs. Thus, a new chapter titled Compensation Scheme for Women Victims/Survivors of Sexual Assault/Other Crimes is added. The POCSO Act, which has its own system and procedures for compensating young victims of sexual abuse, is not covered by this chapter.

It makes it clear that under section 33(8) of the POCSO Act and Rule 7 of the POCSO Rules (now Rule 9 as per updated rules of 2020), only the learned Special Courts are authorized to handle compensation-related matters. Compensation may be provided under the State Victim Compensation Scheme if the child is the victim of an offence other than a sexual one specified under the POCSO Act.

Case study

According to the responses of the Judges in the three states, most of the Judges in most of the cases have recommended the matter to the concerned Legal Services Authority for the grant of compensation. It was stated that in cases that lacked merits, compensation was not granted. The basis for deciding the quantum of compensation was the nature and extent of the injury to the victim, nature of the offence, and the paying capacity of the offender.

Sentencing

The law controls social interests and settles disputes between the citizens' demands and claims. A vital duty of the State is to ensure the safety of its citizens and their possessions. Criminal law serves this purpose by outlining banned behaviour and the penalties for breaking the law. Undoubtedly, there is a cross-cultural clash where the courts must adapt the sentencing system to address new issues and where living law must find solutions. Lawlessness' spread will destabilize society and leave it in ruins. Therefore, the goal of law must be the protection of society and the eradication of criminal propensity, and this goal must be accomplished by imposing the proper penalty. The fact that the legislation uses the word *protection,* raises a reasonable belief that one of the primary intents of bringing such a legislation, though it has not mentioned explicitly, is to prevent or deter child sexual abuse through a strict scheme of punishment, which is reflected in the stricter punishments and mandatory minimum sentences described under the POCSO Act.[47]

Table 4.1 lists out the offences under the POCSO Act along with the punishments that are attached to the said offences.

Punishment scheme for sexual offences under the IPC (Table 4.2).

Prior to its change in 2013, the IPC allowed judges to impose sentences that were less severe than the minimum requirements by providing sufficient justification (section 375 IPC). Although this clause was obviously intended to account for differences in the circumstances and the culpability of those who were charged, its application was frequently marred by patriarchal ideals and excessive compassion for the criminal.[48] The Crime in India statistics of NCRB (2021) reveals that in POCSO offences the conviction rate is 32.2%. The courts have consistently considered the *aggravating factors* on one hand such as the grievousness of the crime, fiduciary relationship between the victim and the perpetrator, and *mitigating factors* such as the young age of the accused and sometimes the financial condition of the accused, etc., on the other hand while giving a sentence in POCSO cases. The judicial decisions given in POCSO cases have been discussed in the subsequent chapter in this book.

Case study

The study conducted in the states of Odisha, Jharkhand, and West Bengal revealed that most of the Judges believed in the rationale of deterrence while awarding a sentence of POCSO. They were of the view that an offence under the said Act was a social evil and the harshest of the punishment should be given to the offender that creates an example to deter prospective offenders. Therefore, the pronouncement of the sentence was made on such lines so as to set an example for the society and deter the probable offenders.

Table 4.1 List of offenses and punishment under the POCSO Act

Section	Offence	Punishment
4	Penetrative sexual assault	Imprisonment for 7 years up to life
6	Aggravated penetrative sexual assault	Rigorous imprisonment for 10 years up to life and fine
8	Sexual assault	Imprisonment for 3 years up to 5 years
10	Aggravated sexual assault	Imprisonment for 5 years up to 7 years
12	Sexual harassment	Imprisonment up to 3 years and fine
14(1)	Using the child for pornographic purposes-	Imprisonment up to 5 years and fine Second conviction- Imprisonment up to 7 years
14(2)	-and committing the offence of penetrative sexual assault	Imprisonment for not less than 10 years upto life and fine
14(2)	- and committing the offence of aggravated penetrative sexual assault	Rigorous imprisonment for life and fine
14(2)	- and committing the offence of sexual assault	Imprisonment for 6 years up to 8 years and fine
14(2)	- and committing the offence of aggravated sexual assault	Imprisonment for 8 years up to 10 years and fine
15(1)	Storage of pornographic material involving a child- - fails to delete or destroy	Fine up to Rs. 5,000 Subsequent offence- Fine up to Rs. 10,000.
15(2)	or report the same to the designated authority	Imprisonment up to 3 years and fine
15(3)	- for the purposes of displaying or distributing in any manner - a child for commercial purposes	Imprisonment for 3 years up to 5 years with fine Subsequent conviction- Imprisonment for 5 years up to 7 years with fine
17	Abetment of an offence u/ the Act	Punishment provided for that offence.
18	Attempt to commit an offence u/the Act	Punishment for a description provided for the offence up to "one-half of the imprisonment for life, one-half of the longest term of imprisonment provided for that offence with fine"
21	Failure to report or record a	Imprisonment up to 6 months with fine
21	case- -Any person - Any person in charge of an institution	Imprisonment up to 12 months with fine
22 (1)	False complaint/ false information regarding offences u/s 3, 5, 7, 9 of the Act	Imprisonment up to 6 months with fine
22(3)	False complaint/ false information for victimizing the child	Imprisonment up to 12 months with fine
23	Violations on part of the media	Imprisonment for 6 months up to one year and fine

Table 4.2 Rape and its punishment under the IPC

Section	Offence	Punishment
376	Punishment for rape	Rigorous imprisonment of not less than ten years up to life imprisonment and fine or both
376(2)	Punishment for aggravated forms of rape	Rigorous imprisonment of not less than ten years up to life imprisonment and fine or both
376(3)	Rape of a woman less than 16 years of age	Rigorous imprisonment of not less than twenty years up to life imprisonment and fine or both
376A	For causing death or resulting in a persistent vegetative state of a victim	Rigorous imprisonment of not less than twenty years up to life imprisonment or death penalty and fine or both
376AB	For rape on a woman under 12 years of age	Rigorous imprisonment of not less than twenty years up to life imprisonment or death penalty and fine or both
376B	Sexual intercourse by husband upon his wife during separation	Imprisonment for a term not less than two years, which may extend up to seven years and fine
376C	Sexual intercourse by a person in authority	Rigorous imprisonment for a term not less than five years which may extend up to ten years and fine
376D	Gangrape	Rigorous imprisonment of not less than twenty years up to life imprisonment and fine
376DA	Gang rape on a woman under 16 years of age	Life imprisonment and fine
376DB	Gang rape on a woman under 12 years of age	Life imprisonment or death penalty and fine
376E	Punishment for repeat offenders	Life imprisonment

Best practices from other countries

Some of the best practices in the State of California, USA, that have led to a heightened sense of awareness among its stakeholders and effective handling of sexual abuse cases that have impacted positively on the trial process may be summed up as follows:

1. California has state-of-the-art crime labs which utilize statewide stand-ardized evidence collection procedures, including uniform rape kits[49] and DNA collection techniques that have been highly effective in resolving rape and sexual assault cases using local, state, and nationwide databases like the Combined DNA Indexing System (CODIS).[50]

2.   California Evidence Code Section 1108, which allows a court to consider prior convictions for sexual offenses, as evidence of an accused's guilt in a subsequent rape or sexual assault prosecution under the 3 strike laws (career offender or repeat offender laws).[51]

3.   Pre-sentence reports or sentencing memoranda that provide the sentencing judge with both aggravating and mitigating information about the offenders so that an appropriate sentence can be imposed.[52]

4.   California Penal Code under section 667.61 California Criminal Code contains the one-strike rape laws that were enacted in 1994, any person convicted of specified sex crimes when certain aggravating factors are present will automatically receive an enhanced sentence of 15 years, 25 years, or life in state prison, depending on the crime combined with the aggravating circumstances. The increase stringency and gravity of sentencing under the one-strike rape laws is considered as one of the major reasons for the reduction in the incidence of sexual assaults/rape (that fall in the category of violent crimes) in the State of California.[53]

In the United Kingdom there are mandatory Sentencing Guidelines that a sentencing judge has to consider at the time of passing the sentence. For repeated rape of the same victim over a course of time or rape involving multiple victims, attracts the highest guideline sentencing levels – 13–19 years. The Sentencing Council's view is that those levels should be available to judges when sentencing for a single rape and the proposed guideline reflects that view.[54]

Conclusion

Justice must not only be done, but must also be seen to be done. This age-old dictum was pronounced by Lord Hewart, who was the Lord Chief Justice of England at that time in the case of *Rex v. Sussex Justices.*[55] This aphorism becomes even more pertinent in the case of one of the most heinous offences, that of a sexual offence that too against one of the most vulnerable groups, that is against a child. The idea of Special Courts to deal with cases of sexual offences against children is to accord a special touch to all aspects of the case during the prosecution and trial stage. Therefore, firstly, it is expected that the courts shall create a child-friendly environment while taking the testimony of the child victim and ensure that the pro-victim safeguarding provisions are complied with. Secondly, the testimony of the child and the trial of these cases should be speedy as the delay dilutes the memory and also the motivation of the victim. In spite of designated Special Courts for trying POCSO cases, the pendency rate of 92% according to the 2021 NCRB data is worrying.

The more effective the participation of the victims in the trial process, the better results can be achieved by the Special Courts. From our case studies, it is revealed that most of the victim-friendly procedures are being complied with, which spells the efficacy of the Special Courts. The data collected shows that on an average the time taken to complete a trial of POCSO is around one year where the average conviction rate is also less than 35%.[56] Also, though the aim of the POCSO Act is to facilitate the child victim and make the journey through the criminal justice process smooth and comforting, the absence of a vertical system of dealing with such cases exposes the vulnerable victim repeatedly to the hostility of the process. Although the victims can be given relief from repeating their stories by recording their statements through audio-videographic modes, from our data collection we find a mixed response to the use of this technology. The underlying principle of audio-video recording of the statements of witnesses by police is to accurately collect and preserve the evidence in the most transparent and efficient manner.[57] Recording of the statement in audio-video mode of the witnesses reduces the instance of cross-examination, thereby providing legitimacy to the statement of the person[58] and in the case of sexual offence victims, it relieves the victim from hostility of recounting her traumatic experience and the harassing cross-examination.

The general mandate to hold the trial of sexual offence cases in-camera and maintain the anonymity of the victim of rape under Section 327(2) of CrPC has not seen very strict compliance and that is why there are directions of the Supreme Court to follow the mandates. This is especially significant in the case of child victims and the POCSO Act (u/s.33) where the Special Court has to ensure that the child's identity is protected at all times throughout the course of investigation or trial.

The other aspects of CSA cases that need to be effectively handled is to see how the courts can rely upon forensic evidence with available resources by properly collecting, storing, and reporting of forensic samples. It is the duty of the courts to see that the victim of CSA is rehabilitated and using the compensation provisions liberally is within the domain of the courts. The POCSO Act provides a very stringent punishment; therefore, the low conviction rate is proof of the fact that the courts require a higher standard of proof to come to a finding of guilt. However, the attitude of the judges from the case study in the three states reveals that there is a tendency to create an example through the sentencing in cases of conviction.

Notes

1 Artinopoulou, V., Koufouli, A., Michael, I. (2018). Towards a victims-centered police response. Training Manual, EU-funded project 'PROTASIS – Police Training Skills'. Athens: European Public Law Organisation [URL: https://protasis-project.eu/protasis-training-manual/].

2 Harford, K.-L. (2008). Psychological consequences of child sexual abuse and the risk and protective factors influencing these consequences. *Dissertation Abstracts International: Section B: The Sciences and Engineering, 68*(12-B), 8398. http://

search.ebscohost.com/login.aspx?direct=true&db=psyh&AN=2008-99120-081 &site=ehost-live.

3 Centre for Child and the Law- National Law School of India University (CCL-NLSIU). (2018). Implementation of the POCSO Act, 2012 by Special Courts: Challenges and Issues. https://ccl.nls.ac.in/wp-content/uploads/2017/01/ Implementation-of-the-POCSO-Act-2012-by-speical-courts-challenges-and-issues -1.pdf.

4 (Patkar, P., & Kandula, P. (2016). 4 YEARS SINCE POCSO Unfolding of the POCSO Act In the State of Maharashtra. http://aarambhindia.org/wp-content/ uploads/2018/05/DigitalAarambh_4-Years-Since-POCSO.pdf)

5 Sharma, P., Unnikrishnan, M. K., & Sharma, A. (2015). Sexual violence in India: Addressing gaps between policy and implementation. *Health Policy and Planning, 30*(5), 656–659. https://doi.org/10.1093/heapol/czu015.

6 Jaiwal H, "Indian Legal Position on Child Sexual Abuse: A Brief Analysis," 2019. Available at https://www.legalserviceindia.com/legal/article-5383-indian-legal -position-on-child-sexual-abuse-a-brief-analysis.html.

7 Section 28 POCSO Act 2012- Designation of Special Courts.

8 Section 32 POCSO Act 2012- Special Public Prosecutors.

9 Section 36 of the POCSO Act- Child not to see the accused at the time of testifying.

10 Centre for Child and the Law- National Law School of India University (CCL-NLSIU), 2018.

11 The Vidhi Centre for Legal Policy (also known as "Vidhi") is a non-profit think tank that conducts legal research to strengthen governance and create better laws for the general welfare. They accomplish this by conducting excellent, peer-reviewed original legal research, collaborating with the Indian government, state governments, and other public institutions to effectively transform policy into law, and engaging in strategic litigation to petition courts on crucial legal and policy issues. Available at https://vidhilegalpolicy.in/about/

12 Sakshi. (2017, January 3. What is special about special courts? The Hindu, January. https://doi.org/10.1037/a0002188)

13 Ibid.

14 Press Trust of India. (2019, July 25). POCSO case: Supreme Court orders setting up of centrally funded special courts in each districts. India Today, 1–12. https://www .indiatoday.in/india/story/pocso-case-supreme-court-orders-setting-up-of-centrally -funded-special-courts-in-each-districts-1573624-2019-07-25

15 Shah, C. (2022). Three years after SC order no additional POCSO courts set up in Mumbai, Thane, Pune. Hindustan Times, 1–11. https://www.hindustantimes.com/ cities/others/three-years-after-sc-order-no-additional-pocso-courts-set-up-in-mum-bai-thane-pune-101664044891685.html

16 Salve, P. (2020, December). What's Slowing Down India ' s Fast-Track Courts. *IndiaSpend*, 1–16. https://www.indiaspend.com/police-judicial-reforms/whats -slowing-down-indias-fast-track-courts-700397

17 Agarwal, Y. (2020, October). Why have Fast Track Courts Failed in India? *The Leaflet*. https://theleaflet.in/why-have-fast-track-courts-failed-in-india/

18 Bajpai, G. S., & KP, S. (2019, April 24). Slow fast-track courts. *Deccan Herald*, 1–24. https://www.deccanherald.com/opinion/main-article/slow-fast-track-courts -730501.html

19 Salve, P. (2020, December). What's Slowing Down India ' s Fast-Track Courts. *IndiaSpend*, 1–16. https://www.indiaspend.com/police-judicial-reforms/whats -slowing-down-indias-fast-track-courts-700397

20 *supra note* 17.

21 Criminal Appeal (DB) No. 196 of 2022.

22 2022 (5) BLJ 302.
23 (2019)20 Supreme Court Cases 196.
24 Section 25 of the POCSO Act 2012- Recording of the statement by the Magistrate.
25 Section 26 of the POCSO Act 2012-Additional provisions regarding statement to be recorded.
26 Section 33 of the POCSO Act- Procedure and powers of the Special Court.
27 CRIMINAL BAIL APPLICATION NO. 3242 OF 2019.
28 The Economic Times. (2022, December 10). Average time taken to dispose of POCSO case is 509 days : Smriti Irani. The Economic Times, 1–15. https://economictimes.indiatimes.com/news/india/average-time-taken-to-dispose-of-pocso-case-is-509-days-smriti-irani/articleshow/96131822.cms?from=mdr
29 Section 309 CrPC – Power to postpone or adjourn proceedings.
30 Section 3- Indian Evidence Act 1872- Interpretation Clause – "Evidence."
31 Kumari, N. (2020). Forensic Evidence and Their Admissibility. *International Journal of Legal Science and Innovation*, 2(2), 769–775. chrome-extension://efaidnbmnnnibpcajpcglclefindmkaj/https://www.ijlsi.com/wp-content/uploads/Forensic-Evidence-and-Their-Admissibility.pdf.
32 M Durga Prasad, Spl Assistant, Syndicate Bank and etc v. The State of AP and etc. [2004 CrLJ 242].
33 Ibid.
34 CRIMINAL APPEAL NO. 1221 OF 2004 decided on April 29, 2009.
35 2009 CrLJ 3039.
36 http://dfs.nic.in/pdfs/IO%20-Forensic%20evidence-Guidelines%20for%20%20IO.pdf
37 Statement of Objects and Reasons, DNA Technology (Use and Application) Regulation Bill, 2018 available at https://prsindia.org/billtrack/prs-products/prs-legislative-brief-3237
38 "Report No. 271: Human DNA Profiling- A draft Bill for the Use and Regulation of DNA-Based Technology," Law Commission of India, July 2017, available at http://lawcommissionofindia.nic.in/reports/Report271.pdf
39 DNA Technology Bill withdrawn from Lok Sabha New Delhi | July 25, 2023 04:02 IST, available at https://indianexpress.com/article/india/dna-technology-bill-withdrawn-from-lok-sabha-8858345/
40 Section 357 CrPC – Order to pay compensation.
41 Gupta Sandhya. (2019). Compensation to Rape Victims- A Critical Analysis. The Criminal Law Blog by National Law University, Jodhpur. https://criminallawstudiesnluj.wordpress.com/2019/08/30/compensation-to-rape-victims-a-critical-analysis/ .
42 Sec. 357A CrPC- Victim Compensation Scheme.
43 Compensation Scheme for Women Victims/Survivors of Sexual Assault/other Crime 2018.
44 W.P. (CRL) 1419/2020 (Date of decision May 13, 2021).
45 Writ Petition (Crl.) 3244/2019, dated 15th June 2020.
46 Writ Petition (Civil) No. 565/2012) (2019) 13 SCC 715.
47 Centre for Child and the Law- National Law School of India University (CCL-NLSIU), 2018.
48 Ibid.
49 Sexual Assault Kits/Evidence FAQs, available at https://oag.ca.gov/bfs/prop69/faqs-sake (visited on August 14, 2023).
50 Frequently Asked Questions on CODIS and NDIS, available at https://www.fbi.gov/how-we-can-help-you/dna-fingerprint-act-of-2005-expungement-policy/codis-and-ndis-fact-sheet (visited on August 13, 2023).

51 Legislative Analyst's Office, The Three Strikes and You're Out Law, February 22, 1995, available at https://lao.ca.gov/analysis_1995/3strikes.html (visited on August 12, 2023).
52 Pre-Sentence Investigation and Report, available at https://www.cacd.uscourts.gov /sites/default/files/attachments/pre-sentence-investigation-and-report.pdf (visited on August 14, 2023).
53 Magnus Lofstrom and Brandon Martin, "Crime Trends in California," available at https://www.ppic.org/publication/crime-trends-in-california/
54 About Sentencing Guideline. https://www.sentencingcouncil.org.uk/sentencing -and-the-council/about-sentencing-guidelines/ (visited on August 14, 2023).
55 [1924] 1 KB 256.
56 Crime in India statistics, National Crime Records Bureau.
57 B.P. Boetig, D.M. Vinson and B.R. Weidel, "Revealing Incommunicado: Electronic Recording of Police Interrogations." *FBI Law Enforcement Bulletin*, 75, no. 12 (2006): 0–8.
58 D.L. Elm and S. Broderick, "Third-Party Case Services and Confidentiality." *Criminal Justice*, 29, no. 1 (2014): 15–40.

5 Judicial approach in cases under the POCSO Act 2012

Introduction

This chapter aims at highlighting the judgements of the POCSO Act 2012 of various different High Courts. Further, this chapter will provide a thorough analysis of various POCSO judgements categorized under different issues that are dealt under the said Act. In this chapter the decisions of the Courts dealt under various aspects of the POCSO Act have been discussed under different heads as follows:

1. Reporting of the offence
2. Recording of the statement of the victim
3. Medical examination of the victim
4. Evidentiary value of forensic evidence
5. Consensual romantic relation between adolescents
6. Burden of proof
7. Sentencing of the accused
8. Compensation to the victim
9. Technicalities of the Act

Reporting of the offence

The State of Maharashtra vs. Maroti[1]

The accused was a medical practitioner appointed for the treatment of girls in a hostel and the victims were taken to him. The residents of the hostel were exploited sexually by five unidentified perpetrators along with the concerned medical practitioner. The FIR was registered against five unidentified perpetrators on the accusation of commission of sexual offence against the minor tribal. The sixth accused was the medical practitioner who aided the other accused, exploited the victim himself, and failed to report the commission of the offence under the POCSO Act in compliance with the legal obligation u/s 19(1) of the POCSO act punishable u/s 21(1) of the POCSO Act. The FIR was registered for the offences u/s 376AB of IPC, Section 4 and 6 of POCSO

DOI: 10.4324/9781003345244-5

Act, Section 3(1)(w) and 3(2)(v) of the Scheduled Castes and Scheduled Tribes (Prevention of Atrocities) Act, 1989 and Section 3 of the Maharashtra Prevention and Eradication of Human Sacrifice and other Inhuman, Evil and Aghori Practices and Black Magic Act, 2013. It was later found that 17 minor girls were abused by the accused medical practitioner and the hymen of the victims was found ruptured on their medical examination. The investigation revealed that the doctor had knowledge about the incidents occurring under his supervision. The accused who was under a legal obligation, in terms of the provisions u/s 19(1) of the POCSO Act upon getting the knowledge about committing of an offence under the POCSO Act, to provide such information either to the SJPU or the local police remained silent and did not provide such information to help the perpetrator. The case was investigated and a charge sheet was filed under Sections 363, 366, 376, and 506 Indian Penal Code and sections 3 and 4 of the POCSO Act.

The charge alleged against the medical practitioner accused was proved in the Trial Court. Accordingly the accused were sentenced to 3 years rigorous imprisonment with a fine of Rs. 3,000/- for the offence under Section 363 IPC, 5 years rigorous imprisonment with a fine of Rs. 5,000/- for the offence under Section 366 IPC, 20 years rigorous imprisonment with a fine of Rs. 25,000/- for the offence under Section 376-D IPC, 2 years rigorous imprisonment with a fine of Rs. 2,000/- under Section 506 IPC, and 7 years rigorous imprisonment with a fine of Rs.7,000/- for the offence under Section 4 of POCSO Act. The prosecution filed an appeal before the Supreme Court against the judgement of the High Court.

The Trial Court reappraised the same in the background of the contentions and arrived at the conclusion that the accused had raped the victim number of times after being enticed away by him. In that view of the matter the Supreme Court was of the opinion that the trial Court had rightly arrived at the conclusion on the basis of the prosecution evidence that the accused was involved in the commission of the crime. The judgement of conviction and sentence of the Trial Court was set aside by the High Court and the FIR against the accused was quashed. The Supreme Court held that the FIR carries suspicion of commission of sexual assault and the charge sheet reveals prima facie against the doctor accused in relation to non-reporting of such an offence under the POCSO Act. The Supreme Court mentioned that the High Court should not have embarked upon an enquiry, especially by looking into the statements of the victims recorded as also their teacher to form an opinion regarding the availability of evidence to connect the doctor accused with the crime. But then, non-reporting of sexual assault against a minor child despite knowledge is a serious crime and more often than not, it is an attempt to shield the offenders of the crime of sexual assault. The High Court arrived at the finding of absence of evidence to implicate the respondent in the crime in question upon going through the statements of the victims and also the statement of the teacher of the victims which was absolutely impermissible.

Thus, the High Court was not justified in bringing abrupt termination of the proceedings qua the doctor accused as established by the Supreme Court. The judgement resulting in the quashing of the stated FIR and the charge sheet throttling the prosecution at the threshold without allowing the materials in support of it to see the light of the day cannot be said to be as an exercise done to secure interests of justice, whereas it can only be stated that such exercise resulted in miscarriage of justice. As a result, the decision of the High Court was set aside and the appeal was allowed. The Supreme Court further confirmed the judgement of the Trial Court and upheld the sentence imposed on the accused.

Nihar Ranjitbhai Barad vs. State of Gujarat[2]

The brief facts of the case were that on July 8, 2022, the victim (aged 12 years) had gone to school in the morning and in the evening came back crying and informed her mother that she does not wish to continue going to school again. On further questioning by her mother, she stated that the appellant (a teacher) had moved his hand over the private parts of the victim inappropriately. The victim ran away on finding an opportunity and went with her mother to the principal the next day to complain. It was then found out that the accused was a habitual offender and an abuser of school girls and accordingly the FIR was lodged.

The Gujarat High Court, while refusing bail to the accused teacher, invoked a Sanskrit verse and highlighted the role and impact of a *Guru* in the life of his/her *Disciple*. Justice Samir J. Dave said:

> "*The accused is not a layman, but a teacher. The only career that influences other professions is teaching. It has the power to influence young people's future for the benefit of future generations. The teacher is expected to act as a protector. Such heinous acts would cast a lifelong psychological and emotional impact on the victim. Crimes like this by a person of trust, change the perception of a child to look forward towards life in a positive way. Therefore, the accused deserves no leniency. The accused instead of showing fatherly love, affection and protection to the child against the evils of the society, rather made her the victim of lust.*"

(emphasis original)

Justice Dave also laid emphasis on a Sanskrit Shloka relating to one's 'Guru' (teacher): 'Guru Brahma, Gurur Vishnu; Guru Devo, Maheshwaraha; Guru Saakshat, Para Brahma; Tasmai Sree Gurave Namaha' [Translation of the verse: 'Guru is verily the representative of Brahma, Vishnu and Shiva. He creates, sustains knowledge and destroys the weeds of ignorance. I salute such a Guru.']

TB vs. State of Odisha[3]

In July 2015, while no one else was present in the house, the appellant (father of the victim) embraced the victim and touched different parts of her body including her breasts and private parts. Being petrified by such conduct of her father, she started crying loudly and he left her. But his degrading act did not see a closure as in that very night itself he slept near the victim, undressed her, and inserted his finger into her vagina, for which she cried. When the situation became unbearable, the victim disclosed the unfortunate incidents before her mother during February 2016, for which there was a quarrel between her parents. Later, her mother advised her to report the matter to the police and an FIR was lodged accordingly.

After the completion of the investigation, the charge sheet was filed and trial was conducted. The Trial Court found the appellant guilty under Sections 354/354A(2)/354B/376(2)(f)(i)(k)(n) of the IPC as well as Sections 6 and 10 of the POCSO Act. Thereafter, the appellant preferred a jail criminal appeal against such an order before the High Court.

It was pointed out that the doctor, who examined the victim, found no injury on her person and also no sign or symptom of recent penetrative sexual assault could be traced. However, the Court refuted such contention by observing that the time gap between the incident and the medical examination in such cases is crucial and therefore the mere absence of injury cannot be a factor for which the Court can discard the testimony of the victim altogether. It was also held that Courts must show sensitivity while deciding the effect of delay in lodging of First Information Report (FIR) in cases involving rape of minors.

The Court further mentioned,

> *This degrading act of the appellant stupefies the judicial conscience of this Court as it is unthinkable to even comprehend that in a country where women are traditionally viewed as an incarnation of the God and daughters are worshipped as 'Devi', such heinous acts are being committed by a father. A daughter needs a father to be the standard against which she will judge all men. When the father who is the creator of the girl child and supposed to act as her protector, takes the role of the predator, it would be sheer betrayal of someone's trust and faith and has got serious impact on humanity.*

The Court stressed that in such cases, the trial Courts must give an empathetic view while deciding the effect of delay on the prosecution case as it is not improbable for a family to take time before reporting such incidents to police, especially when the predator is none else than the father of the victim.

> *Their compulsions should be acknowledged by the Courts in an empathetic manner and the judicial institutions must ensure that bare technicalities of*

criminal jurisprudence do not become shackles of victimhood, forcing the victims to silently digest their pain. Hence, delay in lodging FIR in cases of child rape should be taken with much sensitivity and the concerned Courts must judiciously weigh all the surrounding factors which led to such delay. It is nothing but adding a pinch of salt to her injury to discard the otherwise meritorious case of the prosecutrix merely because she failed to knock at the portals of justice in a time-bound manner,

the Court added.

Additionally, the Court also held that the appellant has committed the offence under Section 376(2)(i) as he committed rape on the victim when she was under 16 years of age. Also, he was found guilty under Section 376(2)(k) as the appellant being in a position of control and dominance over the victim committed rape on her.

Similarly, his conviction under Sections 6 and 10 of the POCSO Act was upheld. The Court also declined to reduce the term of imprisonment as handed down to him by the trial Court. Accordingly, the Jail Criminal Appeal was dismissed.

Recording of the statement of the victim

Gulu Santra @ Ghunu Santra vs. The State of West Bengal[4]

The victim girl, aged 12 years, stated that the accused called her from her house on the pretext of supplying grass for cows and she had been to the field responding to his call without any hesitation because the accused was previously known to the victim, being a man of the village living in the same locality of the victim. She graphically provided the description as to how she suffered aggravated penetrative sexual assault in the hands of the accused. The victim girl consistently spoke in her evidence that the accused gagged her face, while taking her to the jute field, and thus she was not provided with any circumstances to raise any alarm. The victim claimed to have received a threat from the accused requiring her not to disclose the incident to anybody else otherwise he would kill her brother. She returned home crying and narrated everything to her mother as to how she had been sexually violated.

The High Court Observed,

The Trial Court put much emphasis upon the testimony of victim girl together with her statement recorded u/s 164 CrPC since it was given by a twelve-year-old girl, and the same formed the basis of conviction after attracting the presumption available u/s 29 of POCSO Act, for no contrary circumstances in denial of the offence having been established by the accused. The evidence given by the Medical Officer is really of an advisory character, given on the basis of symptoms found on examination.

The victim was medically examined twice and both the doctors consistently ruled out the possibility of committing any penetration upon the victim for want of any symptoms being exhibited on her person including her private parts. The doctor coming a step further stated that he did not find any injury on vulva or the vagina. Not even the redness or tenderness was noted by 2nd doctor. The hymen was also found to be intact. It is not possible that because of intervention of delay caused in the medical examination of victim girl, the probable medical evidence found on the person of victim disappeared. So, neither there was evidence suggestive of attempt of rape, nor commission of rape upon the victim girl. Proof of penetrative sexual assault in terms of Section 3 of POCSO Act is must, without which there cannot be any aggravated penetrative sexual assault and that too upon a girl of below twelve (12) years of age. Since the medical evidence of the two doctors did not attract any of the eventualities mentioned in Section 3 of POCSO Act, it was very difficult and doubtful also in such circumstances to believe the version of victim, as testified during trial merely upon consideration of the statement of victim girl given during trial together with her statement recorded u/s 164 Cr.P.C. The oral evidence of victim coupled with her statement recorded u/s 164 Cr.P.C., for the peculiarity of circumstances involved in this case, could not be given precedence to the medical evidence.

When the testimony of victim girl having failed to secure any objective support from the medical evidence given by two doctors, the testimony of victim cannot be taken to be otherwise believable. It was quite impossible to assume that there will be no injury on the person of victim, a twelve-year-old girl, including her private parts in a case, where she claimed to have been subjected to aggravated penetrative sexual assault by accused/appellant, a sixty-year-old man. The oral testimony of victim claiming to have been violated not being supported by the two doctors upon their medical examination, accordingly would render her testimony to be improbable and not natural also. The credibility of such a witness being thus tainted with doubt for the medical evidence of two doctors, it will hardly pave the way for attracting the presumption available u/s 29 of POCSO Act. Therefore, both the conviction and sentence of the Trial Court were declared not sustainable by the High Court. The accused was favoured with an order of acquittal and he was also discharged from his bail bond by the High Court. In POCSO cases the statement of the victim is given utmost importance.

In this case too, the conviction of the accused was done solely on the basis of the statement of the victim complainant by the Trial Court. Though the case was discovered to be falsely implicated by the High Court in the later stage, however, the motive of the victim was not brought to light as to why the victim tried to falsely implicate the accused. There are a number of similar POCSO cases where the statement of the victim is sufficient to determine the guilt of the accused by corroborating with the medical evidence. The statement of the victim plays a vital role but does not supersede the medical examination report. When corroborated with the medical evidence, the statement of the victim/complainant can be enough to convict the accused.

Navin Dhaniram Baraiye (In Jail) vs. State of Maharashtra through P.S.O.[5]

The complainant lodged a report against the accused in the police station on June 18, 2016, stating that on the same day when she was watching television at home at about 4 p.m. her son (one of the victims) had gone to her sister's adjoining house for playing. When she went there, she found that her son was playing with his friend (the second victim), who was the son of the neighbour. It was claimed that when the complainant went again to see her son, upon opening the door she found that her son was lying on the bed with his pants down and that his aforesaid friend was sitting on him and he had also removed his pant. This shocked the complainant and she asked her son's friend (victim no. 2) as to who had taught him to do such an act, upon which the victim no. 2 stated that the accused had taken him to his house to play mobile game and that he had committed sexual abuse upon him. When the complainant asked her son (victim no.1), he also allegedly told her that the accused had committed such an act with him and that too many times over a period of time. Thereafter, the complainant called the mother of victim no. 2 and narrated the incident to her upon which both the ladies went to the house of the accused and told the said facts to the mother of the accused. Thereupon, the accused was given a beating. The complainant called police upon which the police undertook an investigation and registered the FIR on the same day against the accused u/s 377 of the IPC and Sections 3, 4, 5(l) (m) and 6 of the POCSO Act. Upon completion of the investigation, the police submitted charge sheet and the Court framed charge against the appellant on October 17, 2016, for having committed offences under Section 377 of the IPC and also Section 5 (l) and (m) of the POCSO Act.

The victims had been medically examined and their medical examination reports along with forensic reports were also on record before the trial Court.

The IO stated that she did not personally feel that she should make video recording of the statements of the victims. It has nowhere come on record that video recording in the present case was not undertaken because facility of audio-video electronic means was not available. The Court mentioned that if such recording by audio-video electronic means had been made in the present case, it would clearly have been of assistance to the Court while examining the evidence of the solitary child witness who had deposed in support of the prosecution story in the present case. As a result, the evidence of the said child witness had to be analysed by the Court on the basis of his evidence and cross-examination and the evidence of the Police Officer who recorded the statement of the said child witness on 19.06.2016, a day after the FIR was registered on 18.06.2016. On the basis of the evidence and material on record, the Trial Court found that the prosecution had proved its case against the appellant beyond reasonable doubt and on that basis, by the judgment and order, the trial Court convicted and sentenced the appellant.

Aggrieved by the same, the accused filed an appeal in the High Court. The accused was convicted u/s 377 of the IPC (IPC) read with Sections 3 and 4 of the POCSO Act. He was sentenced to rigorous imprisonment of 7 years and fine of Rs.5000/- imposed upon him by the judgement passed by the Court of Additional Sessions Judge, Nagpur (trial Court) in Special POCSO Case. The only evidence in the present case was the statement of the child witness (victim no.1). It was clear that complainant and mother of victim no. 2, were both deposing on information allegedly given by the victims, rendering their evidence as hearsay evidence. There was no other prosecution witness who could support the statement of the child witness (victim no. 1). The medical evidence on record did not show any corroboration of unnatural sexual assault on the victims and the evidence of Police Officers who recorded the statements of the complainant and those of the victims, demonstrated that neither the complainant nor the victims had stated in their first statements made to the Police about the accused having shown obscene videos to the victims. It has also come on record that the victim no.1 did not state to the Police in the first instance that the accused on one occasion had committed anal sex with him in his house or that the accused used to show obscene videos of girls and boys to the victims. This created serious doubt about veracity of the statements made by the child witness and it appears that he has made statements on being told to do so. A proper analysis of the evidence of the prosecution witnesses and the medical evidence brought on record by the prosecution shows that the foundational facts necessary in the present case to raise presumption u/s 29 of the POCSO Act was not established beyond reasonable doubt by the prosecution. A dispassionate analysis of the evidence and material on record also demonstrates that the present case could be a case of false implication or a complete misunderstanding of the situation by the complainant who seemed to jump to conclusions by making allegations against the accused and thereafter making statements in the evidence which were material improvements over her own statements made to the Police. The judgment and order passed by the trial Court was set aside and the accused was acquitted of the charges levelled against him. Consequently, the accused was directed to be released from custody, if not required in any other case.

This case established the significance of recording of statement of victims in POCSO cases in audio-video mode. The submission was made about the necessity of video recording of the statement of child victims in cases under POCSO Act. Section 26 of the POCSO Act provides for certain safeguards while recording the statement of the child witness. The said provision reads as follows:

Additional provisions regarding statement to be recorded:

1. The Magistrate or the police officer, as the case may be, shall record the statement as spoken by the child in the presence of the parents of the child or any other person in whom the child has trust or confidence.
2. Wherever necessary, the Magistrate or the police officer, as the case may be, make take the assistance of a translator or an interpreter, having such qualifications, experience, and on payment of such fees as may be prescribed, while recording the statement of the child.
3. The Magistrate or the police officer, as the case may be, may, in the case of a child having a mental or physical disability, seek the assistance of a special educator or any person familiar with the manner of communication of the child, or an expert in that field, having such qualifications, experience and on payment of such fees as may be prescribed, to record the statement of the child.
4. Wherever possible, the Magistrate or the police officer, as the case may be, shall ensure that the statement of the child is also recorded by audio-video electronic means.

The provision shows that u/s 26(4) of the POCSO Act, video recording of the statement of the child is not mandatory because the words "wherever possible" have been used in the said provision. But it would be certainly advisable that wherever it is possible and provision is available for video recording, the statement of a child victim in cases under the POCSO Act ought to be recorded by audio-video electronic means also. This would work both ways; on the one hand, it would demonstrate that the child is indeed stating facts on his/her own volition and on the other hand it would also show whether the child victim is being prodded or tutored by anybody to make statement before the police. This would be of assistance to the Court while deciding cases under the POCSO Act.

Medical examination of the victim

Rajesh Mukhi vs. State of Odisha[6]

One Rajesh Mukhi was convicted for commission of offences punishable under sections 376(2)(i)/323/307 of the IPC and section 6 of the POCSO Act, 2012, on the allegation that on August 7, 2014, he sexually abused a minor girl and voluntarily caused hurt to Gajapati Nayak, the grandfather of the victim, and had also assaulted him with a lathi on his head with the intention to commit his murder. The victim was playing on a heap of sand along with her friends in her village. The accused came near the victim, caught hold of her, embraced her body, and committed rape on her by inserting his finger into her vagina. While the occurrence was going on the victim, the grandfather of the victim came to the place of occurrence and when he tried to rescue the victim, the accused assaulted him with a lathi for which he sustained injuries.

On the date of lodging of the first information report itself, the victim was sent for her medical examination and the doctor after examining the victim submitted the medical examination report. The IO visited the spot and the accused was taken into custody on the date of lodging of FIR and he was also sent for medical examination. The statement of the victim was recorded u/s 164 CrPC. The High Court observed that

> the Trial Court mainly relied upon the evidence of the victim, her parents and the injured grandfather to conclude that the accused indeed inserted a finger into the vagina of the victim and the evidence of her has not been discredited. The Trial Court also placed reliance on the evidence of the doctor, who examined the victim and was pleased to hold that the evidence of the victim was found to be trustworthy and worthy of being relied upon and from such evidence, the prosecution proved the charge u/s 376(2)(i) of the IPC and section 6 of the POCSO Act beyond all reasonable doubts. The accused was sentenced to undergo rigorous imprisonment for twelve years and to pay a fine of Rs.1,000/- (one thousand), in default, to undergo further rigorous imprisonment (R.I.) for one year for the offence under section 376(2)(i) of the IPC and R.I. for one year for the offence u/s 323 of the IPC and both the sentences were directed to run concurrently. No separate sentence was awarded for the conviction of the appellant under section 6 of the POCSO Act in view of the provision under section 42 of the said Act.

The medical examination of the victim determined that there was an attempt of aggravated sexual assault. Based on the medical examination of the victim and the injury report of the respective medical practitioners, it was established beyond reasonable doubt that the accused is guilty under section 6 of the POCSO Act. Further, the accused was convicted on the basis of the medical examination report of the minor victim as well as the grandfather of the victim who was also injured by the accused by the Trial Court.

Umesh Karmali vs. The State of Jharkhand[7]

The accused was charged and tried for offences u/s 376/342/506 IPC and Section 4/8/12 of the POCSO Act. The victim was at a stall from where she was allegedly dragged by the accused to his house and was assaulted. The case was registered against the accused and the chargesheet was submitted to the Magistrate of the trial court.

The medical examination of the victim was conducted and the results aided in the decision making of grant of bail of the accused. The medical examination of the victim was done within 36 hours of the alleged occurrence and it did not indicate any sign of rape upon her nor any bodily injury. It was found by the doctor who examined her that there were no signs of any bodily indication of rape or any kind of physical assault. Contending the medical examination reports to be accurate as it was done within 36 hours of the alleged offence the accused was granted bail by the trial court. Having regard these facts and circumstances of the case, the accused named Umesh Karmali was directed to be released on bail on furnishing bail bond of Rs.10,000/-.

The medical examination of the victim helped in determining several charges against the accused to be false.

Manoj Mishra @ Chhotkau vs. The State of Uttar Pradesh[8]

The father of the victim filed a written report before the police alleging therein that one Ramasre alias Siri had enticed his daughter aged about 14 years and had taken her away. In the said complaint, it was further alleged that Raksharam, Nangodiya, and Manoj Kumar alias Chhotkau had cooperated with him in the alleged incident. An FIR was lodged in under Sections 363 and 366 IPC and Section 4 of the POCSO Act. The case was investigated and a charge sheet was filed under Sections 363, 366, 376, and 506 of IPC along with Sections 3 and 4 of the POCSO Act. The victim was found by the police along with Ramasre alias Siri. She was brought back and subjected to medical examination. The doctor who examined the victim stated that the victim who was unmarried was fully grown up and on conducting the necessary tests it was seen that the rupture of the hymen was old and she was found to be 24 weeks into her pregnancy. The medical report was exhibited in the Court, which aided the prosecution evidence.

The Supreme Court observed in connection with the age of the victim and her pregnancy that:

In the cross-examination the doctor referred to the age of prosecutrix as 16 to 17 years. Though she has stated that it could be 17 to 18 years as per general variations, no definite opinion to that effect has been given by her. In the cross-examination she has however stated that the pregnancy was of 23 weeks. Though there is marginal variation with regard to the number of weeks mentioned, the pregnancy was not less than 20 weeks and if the same is kept in the backdrop, the statement of the prosecutrix that the accused had intercourse with her for the first time, four months earlier and that she became pregnant would coincide with the period. In such circumstance, the evidence of the victim and the medical evidence would establish the charge of rape. The Court had thereafter framed the charges against the accused for offence u/s 363, 366 IPC and Section 4 of POCSO Act. On the accused denying the charge, trial was conducted

The Trial Court having analysed the said evidence of the prosecution along with the medical evidence and taking into consideration the denial put forth by the accused while recording the statement under Section 313 of CrPC arrived at the conclusion that the charge alleged against the accused was proved. Accordingly, the accused were sentenced to 3 years rigorous imprisonment with a fine of Rs. 3,000/- for the offence under Section 363 IPC, 5 years rigorous imprisonment with a fine of Rs. 5,000/- for the offence under Section 366 IPC, 20 years rigorous imprisonment with a fine of Rs. 25,000/- for the offence under Section 376-D IPC, 2 years rigorous imprisonment with a fine of Rs. 2,000/- under Section 506 IPC, and 7 years rigorous imprisonment with a fine of Rs. 7,000/- for the offence under Section 4 of the POCSO Act.

The accused assailed the said judgement before the High Court in Criminal Appeal and the Judge while adverting to the evidence tendered before the trial Court and the medical examination report reappraised the same in the background of the contentions that were urged and arrived at the conclusion that the accused had raped the victim number of times after being enticed away by him. In that view of the matter the High Court was of the opinion that the trial Court had rightly arrived at the conclusion on the basis of the prosecution evidence that the accused was involved in the commission of the crime. The judgement of conviction and sentence was accordingly confirmed. The accused therefore claiming to be aggrieved by the judgement passed by the Judge of the High Court filed an appeal before the Supreme Court. The Supreme Court concluded that the victim was raped by the accused number of times after being enticed away by him and also a number of times prior to the incident. The truthfulness or reliability of her statement is undoubtful and there is nothing which may negate the acceptance of her testimony.

The other three accused apart from the accused convicted are the siblings and their father Raksharam has been acquitted by the trial court. In that circumstance, the charge of gang rape has not been established with convincing evidence. However, having already noted that the incident of rape alleged had been established, it would be a case to convict the accused under Section 376 of IPC. However, the conviction handed down by the trial court and confirmed by the High Court u/s 363 and 366 and u/s 4 of the POCSO Act and the sentence as ordered would not call for interference as mentioned by the Supreme Court. As a result, the Supreme Court confirmed the conviction and sentence under Sections 363 and 366, and Section 4 of the POCSO Act. The conviction order made by the trial court and confirmed by the High Court under Section 376 D IPC was modified. The accused is instead convicted under Section 376 IPC and is sentenced, for the period undergone. The appeal was accordingly allowed in part by the Supreme Court and the case was thereafter disposed off. In this case, the statement of the victim coupled with the medical examination report was sufficient for the conviction of the accused for the offense u/s 363 and 366 IPC and Section 4 of the POCSO Act. The medical examination report confirmed that the victim has been subject to sexual intercourse and is pregnant from the past 20 weeks. Thus, the medical examination report acts as substantial evidence to convict the perpetrators majorly in rape cases. In this case as well the trial court convicted the accused based on the statement of the victim and the medical examination report produced. The High Court also took the same aspects into consideration while confirming the charges imposed by the trial court. The Supreme Court took into consideration the medical examination report to establish the charge of rape and upheld the conviction of the trial court and High Court. The sentence imposed by the trial court was modified due to the prior imprisonment undergone by the accused for more than eight years during the trial. Apart from the modified statement, the conviction by the trial court and the High Court remained unaltered.

Kajendran vs. Superintendent of Police and others[9]

The Madras High Court observed that when a minor seeks to terminate a pregnancy arising out of a consensual sexual relationship, the registered medical practitioner may not insist on disclosure of the name of the minor for preparing a report under Section 19 of the POCSO Act as sometimes the minor and their guardian may not be interested in proceeding further with the case.

The Court further held that,

> "*It is clear from the above that where a minor approaches a RMP for medical termination of pregnancy arising out of a consensual sexual activity, it is not necessary to insist for the disclosure of the name of the minor in the report that is normally given under Section 19(1) of the POCSO Act. This procedure has to be followed, since there are instances where minor and their guardian may not be interested in proceeding further with the case and to entangle themselves with a legal process. In such instances, such termination of pregnancy can be made without the disclosure of the name of the minor.*"

Evidentiary value of forensic evidence

Bipin Bhoi vs. State of Odisha[10]

The victim, a minor girl aged about twelve years, had gone to take bath to the nearby village tank. The accused came there and lifted her to the bush and there he made her lie down on the ground, removed her underwear, and committed rape on her. While leaving the place of occurrence, the accused threatened the victim to kill her, if she would disclose the matter before anybody. The mother of the victim disclosed the matter before her husband after he returned from his work and then they went to lodge the written report. On the submission of the charge sheet, the accused refuted the charges, pleaded not guilty and claimed to be tried; the session's trial procedure was resorted to prosecute him and establish his guilt.

The High Court was of the view that

> *The Trial Court found the accused guilty of the offences charged based on the forensic and medical examination report along with the statement of the accused. The trial court sentenced him to undergo rigorous imprisonment for ten years and to pay a fine of Rs.25,000/- in default of which the accused was directed to undergo further imprisonment for six months under section 6 of the POCSO Act and rigorous imprisonment for one year for the offence under section 506 (Part-I) of the IPC. Both the sentences were directed to run concurrently. No separate sentence was awarded for the offence under section 376(2)(i) of the IPC in view of the provision under section 42 of the POCSO Act.*

The conviction of the accused was confirmed by the High Court and the sentence imposed by the trial court was upheld by the High Court. The forensic medical examination report played a vital role in determining the guilt of the accused by the Trial Court and for confirmation of the charges by the High Court. Further, the High Court enhanced the victim compensation amount directed by the Trial Court and recommended the case to District Legal Service Authority to conduct inquiry and grant compensation under the Odisha Victim Compensation (Amendment) Scheme 2018.

Paulus Marandi vs. The State of Jharkhand[11]

In this case the bail petition was filed by the accused and the allegation against the accused was that the accused along with the co-accused persons committed gang rape upon the minor victim girl. The accused persons are charged u/s 376(D)/302/201 of the IPC and u/s 8/12 of the POCSO Act, 2012. It was submitted that the allegation against the accused is false. It was submitted that the report submitted at the State Forensic Science Laboratory (SFSL), Jharkhand, shows that though multiple semen profiles have been found on the different attires of the victim, yet the DNA profile extracted from the blood/urethral swab of the accused does not match and this goes to show that the accused has been falsely implicated merely on the basis of suspicion.

The High Court held that

"considering the facts of this case, the accused was granted bail on fur-
nishing bail bond of Rs.25,000/- (Rupees twenty-five thousand) with two
sureties with the condition that he will co-operate with the trial of the
case. Bail was also granted by the HC primarily on the basis of forensic
evidence."

Consensual romantic relation between adolescents

Ashik Ramjan Ansari vs. State of Maharashtra[12]

The brief facts of the case were that the accused and his partner were in a
consensual relationship where the accused appellant was charged under the
POCSO Act. Both the man (25-year-old in 2016) and the girl (17-year-old in
2016) claimed that they were in a consensual relationship. The girl also stated
that under Muslim law, she was an adult due to her Nikah (marriage) with the
accused. The trial court had observed that while the relationship was consensual, the girl was aged 17 years and 5–6 months and a sexual relationship with
her would amount to rape, as a minor's consent is immaterial. The High Court
noted that the evidence clearly established consensual sexual activity, and the
conviction was erroneous.

In this case, the Bombay High Court called for a shift from a punitive
approach towards adolescents' sexuality to one that enables access to sexual
and reproductive health services. Justice Bharti Dangre was of the opinion that
the criminalization of romantic relationships has burdened the justice system,
consuming significant time and resources, while ultimately the victim turns
hostile. It stressed the importance of striking a balance between the protection
of vulnerable classes and those capable of deciding what is right for them.

"The mere apprehension that adolescents would make an impulsive and
bad decision, cannot classify them under one head and by ignoring their will
and wishes. The age of consent necessarily has to be distinguished from the
age of marriage as sexual acts do not happen only in the confines of marriage
and not only the society, but the judicial system must take note of this impor-
tant aspect," the Court observed. The Court noted that the POCSO Act was
meant to combat the sexual exploitation of children and was never meant to
criminalize consensual relationships among adolescents.

Mahesh Kumar vs. State of NCT of Delhi[13]

The present case was a bail petition filed by the applicant who was booked
under the charges of Sections 363/376 IPC ("IPC") and Section 6 of the
POCSO Act. The brief facts of the case are that the prosecutrix and the applicant were involved in a romantic relationship and both were in their adolescent years. They had run away from their home and when found by the police
on the basis of the complaint filed by the sister of the prosecutrix, she was

seven weeks pregnant. During the course of the trial the prosecutrix admitted that she had developed a liking for the applicant and had gone with him out of her own free will. Though there was a confusion as to the age of the prosecutrix, the Court did not go into the depths of the matter. The prima facie case that was made out was that it was a case of teenage love story. The Court was of the opinion,

> *The main character i.e. the present accused is not a criminal, but was merely in love and at the instance of her lady love, being unaware of the nitty-gritties of law, had taken her to a place which was 2200 kms. away from Delhi to lead a peaceful life. The criminal intent of any kind from the record is completely missing as neither of the characters of the story i.e. prosecutrix and accused had switched off their mobile phones so that their location may not be available to the police or to their family. Therefore, this Court repeats that it is not laying down any law, but only notes with caution that in cases such as the present one, the Courts are not dealing with the criminals, but with two teenage individuals who wanted to live their life as they deemed fit being in love. The love of course did not understand or knew the bar of age of consent as the lovers only knew that they have right to love and lead life as they thought fit for themselves.*

(emphasis original)

Therefore, the bail application was allowed by the Court.

Olius Mawiong & anr. vs. State of Meghalaya[14]

This is an application under Section 482 Cr.P.C preferred with a prayer before this Court to invoke its inherent power to set aside the FIR against the petitioner who was charged under Sections 5 and 6 of the POCSO Act. It was alleged by the mother of the prosecutrix that the local police had influenced her to lodge an FIR against the petitioner as the petitioner and the prosecutrix (pregnant) were married and living together despite being less than 18 years of age. It is interesting to note that such marriage had the consent of the family.

It was held by the Court that,

> *the POCSO Act speaks of penetrative sexual assault and aggravated penetrative sexual assault to indicate that an act of sexual penetration inflicted upon a minor will attract the punishment for the same under the relevant provisions of the said Act. However, in a case where other attending factors such as a case of consensual sex or sex within the bond of marriage albeit between persons who are still minors or one of whom is a minor,*

are not considered in the correct perspective, the course or cause of justice may not have been served, but only the letter of the law fulfilled.

(emphasis original)

In the light of the above, this Court was convinced that the case of the petitioners had to be looked at pragmatically, taking the above observations into consideration to give relief to the parties.

Harsh Vibhore Singhal vs. Union of India & Ors[15]

This case was filed by Advocate Harsh Vibhore Singhal in the nature of a Public Interest Litigation (PIL), which challenged the validity of the statutory rape laws that criminalize consensual sex by 16–18-year-olds. A three-judge bench of the Supreme Court, comprising Chief Justice of India D.Y. Chandrachud and Justices J.B. Pardiwala and Manoj Misra, heard the said PIL. The Apex Court, taking note of the PIL, sought a response from the Centre on seeking a direction to decriminalize the law on statutory rape often invoked against 16- to 18-year-old adolescents for indulging in consensual sex. Sex involving less than 18-year-olds may be consensual in fact, if not in law. Hence, enforcement of criminal law must reflect the rights and capacity of such persons to make informed decisions about engaging in consensual sex and their right to be heard in such matters. The petition also delved into the legislative intent of statutory rape law, which is to criminalize such consent of less than 18 years old persons who, despite consent capacities, wilt and succumb to intimidation, deception, inducement, allurement, manipulation, blackmail, misconception of fact, dominance, control, fraud, etc. In view of these decisions, the PIL highlighted:

> *"that while courts have selectively read down or read in statutory rape law with some jurists viewing with benign eyes and others taking a harsher view, law cannot discriminate between adults similarly situated with one breathing freedom while another jailed- both for consensual sex with less than 18. Unequal and disparate treatment based upon judicial discretion violates Art. 14, 19 and 21 besides leading to an unreliable criminal jurisprudence in such matters. The grey area of law-a legislative vacuum - needs to be filled by guidelines on how statutory rape laws would operate by assessment of consent of 16+ to 18-year-olds before indicting the consenting adults.*

(emphasis original)

Burden of proof

Rabi Munda vs. State of Odisha[16]

As per the FIR lodged by the father of the victim, the victim, who was a minor girl aged about twelve years had been to the nearby forest for grazing goats.

When she was grazing the goats the accused suddenly came near the victim finding her alone, made her lie on the ground, tore her frock and undergarments, and forcibly committed rape on her. The victim raised a cry and on hearing her, people who were working in the nearby cultivable fields rushed to the spot, and on seeing them, the accused fled away. The victim narrated about the occurrence before her brother Ganesh, who in turn intimated the same to his parents over phone. Since it was late night, on the next day the father of the victim came to the police station and lodged the written report against the accused.

The victim supported the prosecution case and stated about the commission of rape on her by the accused. The Trial Court accepted the evidence of the victim that she was raped by the accused and her statement has remained unchallenged. Such a statement of the victim was also corroborated by her parent's statement.

Therefore, the prosecution successfully established the charges under section 376(2)(i) and section 4 of the POCSO Act against the accused. The Trial Court judgment and order found the accused, Rabi Munda guilty for commission of offences punishable u/s 376(2)(i) of the IPC and section 4 of the POCSO Act. The Court sentenced him to undergo rigorous imprisonment for ten years and to pay a fine of Rs.5,000/- (rupees five thousand).

Further the High Court also stated that the law is well settled that in a case of rape, onus is always on the prosecution to prove affirmatively each ingredient of the offence like other criminal cases. The prosecution must discharge the burden of proof to bring home the guilt of the accused and this onus never shifts.

The High Court stated that even though the wearing apparels of the victim and the accused along with sealed glass bottles containing the semen and pubic hair of the accused were sent for forensic examination but no forensic examination report has been provided during trial. The prosecution has not proved that the victim was a child at the time of occurrence and that she specifically was under the age of sixteen years. The oral evidence of the victim was not corroborated by the medical examination even though she was examined on the very next day of the occurrence. Since the Prosecution could not establish the case beyond reasonable doubt, the High Court acquitted the accused of the charges under section 376(2)(i) of the IPC and section 4 of the POCSO Act.

In all criminal cases the primary burden to prove the guilt of the accused lies on the prosecution. Similarly, in this case also the prosecution was supposed to establish the guilt of the accused beyond reasonable doubt but the prosecution could not. In addition to that, there was no forensic or medical examination report produced as evidence during the trial. Despite of the absence of these evidences the Trial Court convicted the accused solely based on the statement of the victim. An appeal was filed in the High Court by the accused regarding the conviction order. The High Court held that the accused could not be convicted u/s 376(2)(i) of the IPC and section 4 of POCSO Act on the grounds that the guilt of the accused was not proved beyond reasonable doubt, absence of medical or forensic examination report, and lastly the lack of corroboration of the statement of the victim produced.

Sitaram Das vs. The State of West Bengal[17]

A seven-year-old girl studying in class II of a primary school and addressing accused as 'Dadu' (grandfather), a 55-year-old man, alleged to have suffered aggravated penetrative sexual assault by such accused. The victim girl, while playing in front of her house, was taken away by the accused (a van rick-shaw puller) on his van rickshaw. Ultimately, she was taken to a nearby bush, when the accused committed rape on the victim leaving a bite mark on her cheek. The victim girl returned home crying after the incident and narrated everything to her mother. Police intervened into the matter after receipt of a complaint from the mother/complainant and put up the victim for her medical examination. The police submitted the charge sheet against the accused person u/s 376(2)(i) of IPC read with Section 6 of the POCSO Act. The Trial Court held the accused person to be guilty of the offence under Section 376(2) (i) of IPC and read with Section 6 of the POCSO Act and sentenced him to ten years rigorous imprisonment with a fine of Rs. 10,000.

The High Court lay emphasis on the fact that,

absence of bite mark on the cheek of victim, what was largely focused not only in the FIR but also in the statement of victim recorded under Section 164 Cr.P.C would make the prosecution story improbable by throwing suspicion over it. However, the Trial Court prioritized the testimony of the other witnesses while going ahead with the conviction. The presumption of guilt u/s 29 of the POCSO Act would not be straightaway applicable as a straightjacket formula, where there is absolutely no evidence from the testimony of victim herself, implicating the accused for the offence complained of. In this case the Trial Court appropriately applied section 29 of the POCSO Act in the instant case, when there was nothing established in proof of previous animosity of victim and her parents with the accused suggestive of false implication.

Consequently, the accused was acquitted by the High Court. The order of conviction and sentence are set aside. The accused was set free accordingly.

Sentencing of the accused

Attorney General for India vs. Satish and another[18]

The High Court (Nagpur Bench) had acquitted an accused observing that groping of the breasts of a minor girl over her clothes will not amount to the offence of sexual assault under Section 8 of POCSO. Holding that there should be *skin-to-skin* contact to attract the offence under Section 8 POCSO, the High Court held that the act in question will only amount to a lesser offence of molestation under Section 354 IPC. The Supreme Court set aside the said controversial judgement of the Bombay HC. The Court further stated, *"restricting the meaning of expression touch and physical contact under Section 7 of POCSO to skin-to-skin contact would not only be a narrow and pedantic interpretation but will also lead to an absurd interpretation of the provision. If such an interpretation is adopted, a person who uses gloves or any other like material while physical groping will not get conviction for the offence. That will be an absurd situation. The construction of the rule should give effect to the rule rather than destroying it. The intention of the legislature cannot be given effect to unless a wider interpretation is adopted. The intent of the law cannot be to allow the offender to escape the meshes of the law".* Since the Act does not define "touch" or "physical contact," the dictionary meanings were referred. Act of touch, if done with sexual intent, will be an offence. Most important ingredient is the sexual intent and not the skin-to-skin contact of the child. Sexual intent is a question of fact which is to be determined from every case separately.

State of U P vs. Sonu Kushwaha[19]

In this case, the Trial Court had sentenced the accused to rigorous imprisonment for 10 years for the offence punishable u/s 6 of the POCSO Act (aggravated penetrative sexual assault) and was directed to pay a fine of Rs. 5,000/- (also imposed rigorous imprisonment for seven years for the offence punishable under Section 377 of IPC. For the offence punishable under Section 506 of IPC, he was sentenced to undergo rigorous imprisonment for one year). Partly allowing his appeal, the Allahabad High Court held that he was guilty of the offence of penetrative sexual assault punishable under Section 4 of the POCSO Act and not the offence of aggravated penetrative sexual assault punishable under Section 6 of the POCSO Act. Therefore, his sentence for the offence punishable under the POCSO Act was brought down to imprisonment for seven years with a fine of Rs. 5,000/-.

The Supreme Court further observed that,

the POCSO Act was enacted to provide more stringent punishments for the offences of child abuse of various kinds and that is why minimum punishments were prescribed in Sections 4, 6, 8 and 10 of the POCSO Act for various categories of sexual assaults on children. Hence, Section 6, on its plain language, leaves no discretion to the Court and there is no option but to impose the minimum sentence as done by the Trial Court. When a penal provision uses the phraseology "shall not be less than....", the Courts cannot lessen the offence to the Section and impose a lesser sentence. The

Courts are powerless to do that unless there is a specific statutory provision enabling the Court to impose a lesser. However, we find no such provision in the POCSO Act. Therefore, notwithstanding the fact that the respondent may have moved ahead in life after undergoing the sentence as modified by the High Court, there is no question of showing any leniency to him. Apart from the fact that the law provides for a minimum sentence, the crime committed by the respondent is very gruesome which calls for very stringent punishment. The impact of the obnoxious act on the mind of the victim-child will be lifelong. The impact is bound to adversely affect the healthy growth of the victim. There is no dispute that the age of the victim was less than twelve years at the time of the incident. Therefore, we have no option but to set aside the impugned judgment of the High Court and restore the judgment of the Trial Court.

Md. Israil vs. The State of West Bengal[20]

The accused used to come to the house of the victim for the last seven to eight years and he used to call the victim (aged about 14 years) as "grand-daughter." Taking advantage of the absence of other family members the accused used to come to the victim's house and committed rape on her repeatedly on a number of occasions, which also resulted in her pregnancy. The accused also threatened her not to disclose the fact to anyone, otherwise he would kill the victim and her brother. Finally, the victim lodged a complaint herself against the accused under Section 376(2)(i) of IPC and Section 4 of the POCSO Act, 2012.

The High Court observed that

"the Trial Court convicted the accused and sentenced him for offence u/s 6 of the POCSO Act, 2012 for rigorous imprisonment for life. In the present case, offence of penetrative sexual assault had been committed upon a helpless victim of 14 years which was inhumane and that has shaken the judicial conscience. However, keeping in mind the entirety of the circumstances the quantum of sentence imposed by the trial court for rigorous imprisonment for life in respect of offence under section 6 of the POCSO Act, 2012, which is the maximum one was modified to 14 years of rigorous imprisonment. The Court observed that ordinarily the sentence should commensurate with the gravity of offence and should act as deterrent to commission of such offences. In the present case, a term of 14 years imprisonment is justified. It was found that there was repeated sexual assault upon the victim by the appellant resulting in her pregnancy, which is an aggravating circumstance.

Thus, it was held that under the entire gamut of circumstances a term of 14 years of rigorous imprisonment will be proportionate with the nature of the offence and accordingly sentence for rigorous imprisonment for life imposed in respect of Section 6 of POCSO Act, 2012, is reduced to rigorous imprisonment for a term of 14 years'. The compensation was granted to the victim under the Victim Compensation Scheme.

Vijay Raikwar vs. the State of Madhya Pradesh[21] On 5 February, 2019

The victim of the incident was a minor girl, aged 7 1/2 years. In the same village, the accused also started living for two to three years prior to the date of the incident. On the date of the incident in the evening after the parents of the victim returned home after work, they did not find the victim in the house. On asking the neighbours, the mother came to know that the victim was playing in the house of the accused. When they reached the house of the accused they neither found him nor the victim. They, however, could find the blue frock school uniform of the victim on the cot and blood stains on the bed mattresses. On further search, they found the naked dead body of the victim lying by the side of the road.

The accused was tried by the Trial Court for the offences punishable under Section 376 (2) (f) and Section 201 of the IPC as well as Sections 5(i), 5(m) and 5(r) read with Section 6 of the POCSO Act for having committed the murder of the minor girl aged 71/2 years after raping her. On considering the incriminating material against the accused and on appreciation the evidences and having considered that the accused was last seen together with the deceased and that the frock of the victim was found lying on the cot along with blood stains on bed mattress and bedsheet in the house of the accused, which was not explained by the accused. The medical evidence was also taken into consideration.

The Trial Court convicted the accused for the offences under Section 376 (2) (f) and Section 201 of the IPC as well as Sections 5(i), 5(m) and 5(r) read with Section 6 of the POCSO Act. The Trial Court sentenced the accused to death penalty. Having sentenced the accused with death penalty, the Additional Sessions Judge of the Trial Court made the reference to the High Court. Being aggrieved with the conviction and the sentence, the accused preferred Criminal Appeal before the High Court.

By the common judgment and order, the High Court decided the reference against the accused and also dismissed the criminal appeal preferred by the accused. Further the High Court has confirmed the conviction and sentence imposed by the Trial Court. Feeling aggrieved and dissatisfied with the impugned judgment and order passed by the High Court, the conviction and sentence of death penalty, the accused filed an appeal in the Supreme Court. The Supreme Court contended the facts and circumstances of the case. The accused's contention was that both the courts materially erred in holding him guilty for the offences under Section 376 (2) (f) and Section 201 of the IPC as well as Sections 5(i), 5(m) and 5(r) read with Section 6 of the POCSO Act. He vehemently submitted that there was no eye-witness of the incident and the entire case is based on circumstantial evidence. It was submitted that unless and until the chain of evidence proves the guilt of the accused beyond reasonable doubt in committing the crime, both the courts materially erred in convicting the accused.

The Supreme Court stated that the prosecution was successful in proving that the accused was last seen together with the victim, that he gave one rupee coin to the victim, he told Bharati (sister of the accused and friend of the victim), who was with the victim to go away after which the dead body of the victim was found near the house of the accused, that the frock of the victim was lying on the cot and the bed mattress and bedsheet were blood stained and the same was matched with the blood group of the victim and that the accused failed to explain the incriminating material/evidence found against him in the statement under Section 313 of Cr.P.C.

The Supreme Court further added that the Trial Court rightly convicted the accused which has rightly been confirmed by the High Court. Holding the accused guilty for having committed the murder after raping a minor girl. Thus, the Supreme Court upheld the judgment and order of the conviction passed by the Trial Court, confirmed by the High Court. The gravity of the offence was acknowledged but that did not qualify to fall in the category of "rarest of rare case" warranting the death sentence. The offence committed was brutal but did not warrant death sentence. It was further noted that the accused was not a previous convict or a professional killer. At the time of commission of offence, he was 19 years of age. His jail conduct was also reported to be good. Considering the aforesaid mitigating circumstances and in the interest of justice the Supreme Court decided to commute the death sentence to life imprisonment. His conviction for the offences under Section 376 (2) (f) and Section 201 of the IPC as well as Sections 5(i), 5(m) and 5(r) read with Section 6 of the POCSO Act was confirmed. However as per the facts and circumstances of the case the Supreme Court commuted the death sentence of the accused to life imprisonment.

Compensation to the victim

Bhalu Murmu @ Galu vs. State of Odisha[22]

The mother of the victim filed a complaint before the police where she stated that her daughter who was aged about three years was roaming in a nearby field, where the accused took the victim to his house on the pretext of giving her some food items and thereafter committed rape on her. The victim returned home crying and told the incident to her mother that a person who is having an amputee committed rape on her. The mother took the victim with her to identify the culprit and the victim identified the accused. The mother observed cut injuries on the private part of the victim and the victim was feeling severe pain while urinating. A case was registered under sections 376(2)(i) of the IPC and section 4 of the POCSO Act.

The accused faced trial in the Court for commission of offences punishable under section 376(2)(i) of the IPC and section 6 of the POCSO Act, 2012. The prosecution successfully established the charges beyond all reasonable doubt. The Trial Court found the accused guilty and sentenced him to undergo further R.I. for a period of one year for the offence under section 376(2)(i) of the IPC and rigorous imprisonment for a period of twelve years and to pay a fine of Rs.3,000/- (three thousand), in default, to undergo further R.I. for a period of one year for the offence under section 6 of the POCSO Act.

However, the sentence given by the Trial Court was erroneous and therefore the High Court modified the error and sentenced the accused to undergo R.I. for a period of ten years for the offence under section 6 of the POCSO Act. The fine amount and the default sentence which had been imposed for the offence under section 6 of the POCSO Act by the trial Court remained unaltered. No separate sentence was imposed for the conviction of the appellant under section 376 (2) (i) of the IPC in view of section 42 of the POCSO Act and the conviction was upheld by the Odisha High Court. In view of the Odisha Victim Compensation (Amendment) Scheme, 2018 and keeping in view the age of the victim at the time of occurrence and the nature and gravity of the offence committed and the family background, the High Court recommended the case to DLSA to examine the case of the victim after conducting the necessary enquiry in accordance with law for grant of compensation under the Odisha Victim Compensation (Amendment) Scheme, 2018.

Ali Imam vs. The State of West Bengal & Anr[23]

The mother of the victim filed a written complaint with the police on September 19, 2015, alleging that on the day of the occurrence, his son, the victim aged about 11 years, came home who was mentally disturbed and was crying. The victim boy had narrated an incident that he was coming home from the saloon, the accused, residing at the third floor of the same premises, took him to his flat and kissed the victim boy, made him naked, and sexually abused him. Thereafter, the accused had threatened the victim stating that if the victim disclosed the incident to anybody else he would kill him. The accused was charged under sections 4/8/12 of the POCSO Act, 2012 read with Section 506 of the IPC, 1860. The charges were submitted under Section 506 of the IPC, 1860 read with Sections 4/8/12 of the POCSO Act, 2012.

The accused was found guilty of the charges by the Trial Court. By the order of sentence, the accused was sentenced to suffer rigorous imprisonments for varying periods for the offences he has been found guilty of. He was directed to pay fines of various amounts and in default to undergo rigorous imprisonment. All the sentences had been directed to run concurrently. The victim boy was awarded with compensation in final form of Rs. 50,000 under

Section 357 (2) of the CrPC. The State Legal Services Authority, Government of West Bengal had been directed to pay the compensation amount to the victim boy.

The High Court established beyond reasonable doubt that the accused was guilty of the charges framed against him. Thus, the High Court confirmed the conviction of the accused by the Trial Court and upheld the sentence imposed by the Trial Court. Further, the High Court did not interfere with the judgment of the Trial Court with respect to the compensation to be paid to the victim and directed the payment of compensation as mentioned by the Trial Court.

Baneshwar Marandi @ Boneshwar vs. The State of Jharkhand[24]

One Ranga was charged for the offence under section 376(G) of the IPC and under Section 4 of the POSCO Act on the basis of the written report of the informant alleging when she had gone for taking bath in a waterfall and in her course of bath one Joiten Soren and one Baneshwar Marandi caught the victim and took her towards the forest. The victim could not raise alarm as she was deaf and dumb and thereafter the accused persons raped her one by one and they fled away towards the forest. The victim disclosed the incident to her father by sign language and also showed the house of the accused persons and identified the accused persons by sign. On the basis of these allegations and other allegations, the complaint was lodged against the accused persons.

The offence punishable under sections 376(D) of the IPC and under Section 4 of the POCSO Act, 2012, was framed against the accused. The victim answered by signs related to catching of her hand and pressing of her neck. She also indicated about tying her hands and taking away to their house. On the facts held, the medical evidence however admitted that there was neither any penetration nor any injury over the private part. The evidence only reveals that on hearing the screaming sound of his daughter, the victim's father rushed to the spot, and it is then noticed that the accused was laying on his daughter and attempting to commit rape, but did not succeed and fled away from the place. Therefore, the accused was tried under section 376 r/w Section 511 IPC and section 4 of the POCSO, 2012, in the trial court.

The High Court rejected the bail application of the accused and directed Trial Court the speedy disposal of the case. Further, the Principal District Judge-cum-Chairman, DLSA, Sahibganj was directed to ensure as to whether the compensation of Rs. 3 lakhs were paid to the victim or not. Thereafter the matter was adjourned and Rs, 3,00,000/- was said to the victim in the account of the victim under the Victim Compensation Schemes. As the case involved a minor victim who was both deaf and dumb, this aggravated the nature of the offence. Thus, the victim was compensated Rs.3,00,000 under the victim compensation scheme by the Jharkhand High Court for the rehabilitation of the victim.

X vs. State of NCT of Delhi (Acting Through Its Secretary) & anr[25]

Ordering increase in the amount of compensation for survivors of child sexual abuse from Rs 7 lakh to at least Rs 10.5 lakh under the 2018 Delhi Victim Compensation Scheme, the Delhi High Court on Thursday said that the final compensation to the victims must be the maximum amount as provided in the scheme's schedule. The schedule of the 2018 scheme mentions both minimum and the upper limit of compensation to be awarded to victims. Ordering increase in the amount of compensation for survivors of child sexual abuse from Rs 7 lakh to at least Rs 10.5 lakh under the 2018 Delhi Victim Compensation Scheme, the Delhi High Court on Thursday said that the final compensation to the victims must be the maximum amount as provided in the scheme's schedule.

The schedule of the 2018 Scheme mentions both minimum and the upper limit of compensation to be awarded to victims. Observing that no amount of monetary compensation can undo the trauma undergone by the victim, the court said it is necessary to put money in the hands of the victim and family as the funds will not only provide a sense of safety but also cater to their immediate needs. Observing that the interim compensation must be paid to the victims at the earliest, the court said that while no time frame has been given, however, the amount must be disbursed within a period of two months within the filing of charge sheet.

Technicalities of the Act

State of Kerala vs. Hafsal Rahman N.K.[26]

In this case the accused was the teacher of the victim. The allegation against him was that he touched her cheeks and kissed on her forehead, etc. Following the incident, a complaint was registered for offences punishable under Secs.9(f) and 10 of the POCSO Act, 2012. Before the High Court, the victim filed an affidavit that she has settled the entire dispute with the accused and that she has no objection for quashment of the criminal proceedings pending against him. Recording this, the High Court of Kerala quashed the criminal proceedings.

Before the Apex Court, the state contended that this was not permissible in view of the judgement reported in 2019 (5) SCC 688 titled as *State of Madhya Pradesh vs. Laxmi Narayan*. In the said judgement, it was observed that the power under Section 482 CrPC is not to be exercised in those prosecutions which involve heinous and serious offences of mental depravity or offences like murder, rape, dacoity, etc. Such offences are not private in nature and have a serious impact on society.

Taking note of this, the bench, while issuing notice, stayed the High Court judgement and permitted investigation to continue.

Conclusion

After analysing all the cases under the seven different perspective issues it can be observed that in majority of POSCO cases, the perpetrator usually has a prior relationship or acquaintance with the victim because of which the victim trusts the perpetrator and ends up in a helpless situation. Further, the medical evidence collected from the accused as well as the victim when handled correctly is said to play a vital role in the trial process. The medical evidence corroborated with the oral testimony of the victim and the witnesses is mostly considered as substantial evidence for the conviction of the accused. POCSO cases are always dealt with special care and attention by all the stakeholders of the criminal justice system as it involves the most vulnerable group of the society that being children. Analysing the cases showed that the perpetrators of sexual abuse of children are usually not given any leniency while being tried by the Magistrate. In certain aggravating cases the perpetrator may also be awarded death penalty, which has been observed in many POSCO cases where the offence was heinous enough in nature to sentence the accused death penalty. In addition to that, it is observed that most of the cases are also being referred to the Legal Services Authority for grant of compensation. In certain other situations where the nature of the crime is gruesome enough to shock the consciousness of the society, such victims or the family of the victim in case of the demise of the victim are compensated by the Special Courts under various victim compensation schemes. In the case of recording of statements, it was noticed that while recording the statement of the victim adequate measures were taken as prescribed under various provisions of the POCSO Act and it is assured that the accused does not confess or provide incriminatory statements to the magistrate under any cohesion or non-voluntarily. Forensic evidence plays a very dominant role in establishing the guilt of the perpetrator as well as influences the sentencing of the perpetrator. The courts in applying the reverse burden on the defence requires the prosecution to prove certain foundations facts with respect to the commission of the offence and linking the offender with such offence. POCSO cases are dealt with caution and care by the Courts of India with proper and adequate measures required while trying POCSO cases. It can be concluded that the stakeholders of the criminal justice system take into the best interests of child victims into consideration while trying POCSO cases to protect and secure the future of our Nation by protecting and securing the children of our nation.

Children are the most indispensable and vulnerable group of the society who need care and protection. According to the data from Crime in India statistics NCRB, post the enactment of POSCO Act there has been a drastic increase in reporting of sexual offences against children. The various patterns while delivering judgements in POSCO cases are observed under seven different issues which include the reporting of the offence, the sentencing of the accused, the compensation of the victim, the recording of the statement, the inclusion of forensic evidence, the inclusion of medical evidence, and the concept of burden of proof. Justice to the victim and the rehabilitation of the victim should be the prior goal of the Criminal Justice System so that the child victims of gruesome and heinous crimes get rehabilitated and reintegrated back into the society.

Notes

1 *The State of Maharashtra vs. Maroti*, decided on November 2, 2022 (Supreme Court of India).
2 *Nihar Ranjitbhai Barad vs. State of Gujarat*, 2022 LiveLaw (Guj) 414 (In the High Court of Gujrat at Ahmedabad).
3 *TB vs. State of Odisha* (2023 LiveLaw (Ori) 85).
4 *Gulu Santra @ Ghunu Santra vs The State of West Bengal*, decided on June 12, 2020.
5 *Navin Dhaniram Baraiye (In Jail) vs. State of Maharashtra* through P.S.O, decided on June 25, 2018.
6 *Rajesh Mukhi vs. State of Odisha*, decided on September 7, 2022 (High Court of Odisha).
7 *Umesh Karmali vs The State of Jharkhand*, decided on September 7, 2017 (High Court of Jharkhand).
8 *Manoj Mishra @ Chhotkau vs. the State of Uttar Pradesh*, decided on October 8, 2021 (Supreme Court of India).
9 Case No: HCP 2182 of 2022 (High Court of Tamil Nadu at Madras).
10 *Bipin Bhoi vs. State of Odisha*, decided on July 22, 2021 (High Court of Odisha).
11 *Paulus Marandi vs. The State of Jharkhand*, decided on February 26, 2021 (High Court of Jharkhand).
12 *Ashik Ramjan Ansari vs. The State of Maharashtra* (CRIMINAL APPEAL NO.1184 OF 2019, High Court of Maharashtra at Bombay).
13 *Mahesh Kumar vs. State of NCT of Delhi* (Bail Application No. 1240/2023, High Court of Delhi).
14 *Olius Mawiong & anr. vs. State of Meghalaya* (Crl. Petition of 22 of 2022, High Court of Meghalaya).
15 WRIT PETITION (CIVIL) NO. 000700 OF 2023, Supreme Court of India.
16 *Rabi Munda vs. State of Odisha*, decided on September 13, 2021 (High Court of Odisha).
17 *Sitaram Das vs. The State of West Bengal*, decided on February 27, 2020 (High Court of west Bengal).
18 *Attorney General for India vs. Satish and another*, LL 2021 SC 656.
19 *State of U.P. vs. Sonu Khushwaha*, 2023 LiveLaw (SC) 502 | CrA 1633 OF 2023.
20 *Md. Israil vs. The State of West Bengal*, decided on February 2, 2022 (High Court of West Bengal).
21 *Vijay Raikwar vs. the State of Madhya Pradesh*, decided on February 5, 2019 (Supreme Court of India).
22 *Bhalu Murmu @ Galu vs. State of Odisha*, decided on August 5, 2021 (High Court of Odisha).
23 *Ali Imam vs The State of West Bengal & Anr*, decided on August 1, 2022 (High Court of West Bengal).
24 *Baneshwar Marandi @ Boneshwar vs. The State of Jharkhand* on December 4, 2018 (High Court of Jharkhand).
25 *X vs. State of NCT of Delhi (Acting through its secretary) & anr.*, 2022 LiveLaw (Del) 996.
26 *State of Kerala vs. Hafsal Rahman N.K*, SPECIAL LEAVE PETITION (CRIMINAL) Diary No(s). 24362/2021 (Supreme Court of India).

Index

For Product Safety Concerns and Information please contact our EU
representative GPSR@taylorandfrancis.com
Taylor & Francis Verlag GmbH, Kaufingerstraße 24, 80331 München, Germany